Best Poems of 1972

FOREWORD

Best Poems of 1972 presents the Borestone selections of poems first published in the year 1972 in magazines of the English-speaking world. The magazines and the issues from which the selections were made are listed in the "Contents." Poems in the late winter issues that are not available for reading before the close of the year will be considered for next year's selections. By the time the compilation is completed in early 1973, some of the selections are scheduled for reprinting in collections of the poets. These subsequent reprintings and other recognitions are recorded under "Acknowledgments and Notes."

The few requirements established for the first volume have never been changed. A poem is eligible if it is the first printing and not over one hundred lines. Translations, unpublished poems, and reprints from other publications and books are not considered.

The editorial procedure has also been consistent throughout the twenty-five volumes. Some three hundred or more poems are selected by the reading staff each year. When the year's selections are complete, copies of the poems are sent to the judges with the names of the authors and periodicals deleted, as there is no intention of recognizing established names in preference to newcomers, or apportioning selections between periodicals and countries. The judges score their individual preferences and forward the results to the office of the Managing Editor, where a tabulation of the scores determines the final selections. The three highest scores are the winners of the year's awards. Thus, there can be more than one poem by the same poet and a number of poems from the same periodical.

"Advent" by Noel Welch received the first award of $300. "In the Face of Descent" by T. Alan Broughton won the second award of $200, and "Seven Preludes to Silence" by Richard Shelton received the third award of $100.

The editors gratefully acknowledge permission to reprint these selected poems from the magazines, publishers, and authors owning the copyrights.

The Editors

Lionel Stevenson
Chairman
Howard Sergeant
*British Commonwealth
Magazines
(except Canada)*

Hildegarde Flanner
Frances Minturn Howard
Gemma d'Auria
Waddell Austin
Managing Editor

ACKNOWLEDGMENTS AND NOTES

"Seven Preludes to Silence" by Richard Shelton, selected from the original printing in the March 4, 1972 issue of *The New Yorker*, appears in his collection of poems, *Of All the Dirty Words*, copyright © 1972 by the University of Pittsburgh Press and reprinted by their permission.

"The Heir" by Jeni Couzyn was first published in *Workshop* (England) and subsequently included in her collection of poems, *Monkey's Wedding*, copyright © 1972 by Jeni Couzyn, and published by Jonathan Cape, London.

"Return" by Patricia Cumming is from the original printing in the Winter 1972 issue of *Shenandoah*, copyright © 1972, and is reprinted by permission of the Editor of *Shenandoah: The Washington and Lee University Review*.

The poems "Clouds," "Losing You," "Parabola," and "Scorpion" appeared in 1972 issues of *Poetry*, copyright © 1972 by The Modern Poetry Association, and are reprinted by permission of the Editor of *Poetry*.

"The Children" by Harley Elliott is from the original printing in the Fall 1972 issue of *Minnesota Review*. The poem will be included in his second book, *All Beautyfull and Foolish Souls*, to be published by The Crossing Press in October 1973.

"The Coat" by Peter Everwine, originally from *The New Yorker*, is included in his book, *Collecting the Animals*, copyright © 1972 by Peter Everwine, and reprinted by permission of Atheneum Publishers.

"Orestes" by Robert Fagles is from the Summer 1972 issue of *The Yale Review*, copyright © 1972 by *The Yale Review*.

"When This Ends, And It Will" by Barbara Harris is from the original printing in the Spring 1972 issue of *The Southern Review*. Barbara Harris died in 1964. The poem was submitted to *The Southern Review* by her friend, Ann Stanford.

"Stones" by Maxine Kumin has subsequently been included in her collection, *Up Country: Poems of New England*, copyright © 1972 by Maxine Kumin, and is included in the Borestone selections by permission of Harper & Row, Publishers, Inc.

"Survival Story" by Wes Magee, selected from the Spring 1972 issue of *Prism International*, was also published in the Spring issue of *Poetry of the Circle in the Square* (England).

"Lightning Bugs" by Frank Manley was copyrighted © 1972 by *Partisan Review*.

"Old Voices" and "Bridges" by Leslie Norris are copyrighted © 1972 by *The Atlantic Monthly* and held in trust for the author.

"Søren" by John Peck was subsequently included in his collection of poems, *Shagbark*, copyright © 1972 by John Frederick Peck, and reprinted by permission of the publisher, The Bobbs-Merrill Company, Inc.

"The Beautiful Acceptance" by Richard Pevear is reprinted by permission of *The Hudson Review* and copyrighted © 1972 by The Hudson Review, Inc.

The *Northwest Review* has assigned the copyright to Stanley Plumly for his poem, "For J., Ardea Occidentalis."

"Love in an Earthquake" by Jarold Ramsey subsequently became the title poem in his new collection, *Love in an Earthquake*, published by the University of Washington Press, Seattle, 1973. Permission to reprint is from the University of Washington Press.

"The Goose-Girl" by Campbell Reeves, selected from the original printing in the 1972 special issue of *Southern Poetry Review*, is included in her collection of poems, *Coming Out Even* (May 1973), and is reprinted by permission of Moore Publishing Company, Durham, North Carolina.

"A Suicide Pact" by David Schloss has been included in his collection of poems, *The Beloved*, copyright © 1972 by David Schloss, and reprinted here by permission of the author and The Ashland Poetry Press, Ashland College, Ashland, Ohio.

"Scorpion" by Michael Schmidt, originally selected from the February 1972 issue of *Poetry*, has been included in his collection of poems, *Desert of the Lions*, published in 1972 by Carcanet Press (Dufour Editions Inc.) England, and is reprinted by permission of the publisher and the author.

"Lesson in Survival" by Peter Scupham, selected from the original printing in the Spring 1972 issue of *Outposts*, has been included in his collection of poems, *The Snowing Globe*, copyright © by Peter Scupham, and reprinted by permission of Eric & David Morten, Publishers, Manchester, England, and the author.

"The Dead and the Living" by Edward Storey has been included in his second book of poetry, *A Man in Winter,* published in 1972 by the Wesleyan University Press in the United States and by Chatto and Windus Ltd. in England.

"The Possessed" by Mark Van Doren was selected from the first publication in *The Hudson Review,* Vol. XXV, No. 2 (Summer 1972). Mark Van Doren died in December 1972. *The Hudson Review* has assigned copyright to the estate of Mark Van Doren and we gratefully acknowledge Nannine Joseph's permission to include the poem.

"Afterward" by Ted Walker was selected from the original printing in the October 7, 1972 issue of *The New Yorker.* Mr. Walker changed the title to "Afterwards" as it subsequently appears in his collection of poems, *Gloves to the Hangman,* published in May 1973 and reprinted by permission of Jonathan Cape Ltd., London, and the author.

"Childermas hymn: December 28, 1970" by Tom Wayman was subsequently included in his collection of poems, *Waiting for Wayman,* published in the spring of 1973, and is reprinted by permission of McClelland and Stewart Ltd., Toronto, and the author.

"Before the Night" by Theodore Weiss was selected from the first printing in the September 1972 issue of *Esquire Magazine,* copyright © 1972 by Esquire, Inc.

"Reading the Rites" by Nancy G. Westerfield was selected from Volume 27, No. 4 (Winter 1971–72) issue of *Arizona Quarterly,* copyright © 1972 by *Arizona Quarterly.*

The poems "Seven Preludes to Silence" (page 7), "The Coat" (page 30), "After the Rain" (page 55), "The Mexican Peacock" (page 65), "Søren" (page 93), "Omen" (page 120), and "Afterwards" (page 125) are copyrighted © 1972 by The New Yorker Magazine, Inc.

CONTENTS

Noel Welch: (*First Award*)	Advent	1
	English (England)—Autumn	
T. Alan Broughton: (*Second Award*)	In the Face of Descent	3
	The Beloit Poetry Journal—Spring	
Richard Shelton: (*Third Award*)	Seven Preludes to Silence	7
	The New Yorker—March 4	
Kaywynne Adams:	Wassail	9
	Prairie Schooner—Winter	
Patricia Beer:	After Death	11
	New Statesman (England)—September	
Benjamin K. Bennett:	Socrates	13
	Quarterly Review of Literature—Vol. XVIII, No. 1–2	
Douglas Blazek:	After Walking To & Fro & Up & Down in It	14
	Prism International (Canada)—Fall	
James Blish:	Grand Pause	15
	Prairie Schooner—Summer	
Philip Booth:	Wear	16
	Poetry Northwest—Winter	
R. F. Brissenden:	Building a Terrace	18
	Westerly (Australia)—June	
Hayden Carruth:	The Ushers	20
	Quarterly Review of Literature—Vol. XVIII, No. 1–2	
Jeni Couzyn:	The Heir	23
	Workshop New Poetry (England)—No. 16	
Patricia Cumming:	Return	25
	Shenandoah—Winter	
Stephen Dobyns:	Clouds	26
	Poetry—March	
Carleton Drewry:	Stillborn	27
	Southwest Review—Winter	
Harley Elliott:	The Children	29
	Minnesota Review—Fall	
Peter Everwine:	The Coat	30
	The New Yorker—September 23	
Robert Fagles:	Orestes	31
	The Yale Review—Autumn	

Norma Farber:	High Torque	32
	Counter/Measures—No. 1	
Norma Farber:	Looking at the Coelacanth	33
	Satire Newsletter—Vol. IX, No. 2—Spring	
Norma Farber:	Theory of Flight	34
	Poetry Northwest—Spring	
Roy Fuller:	On His Sixtieth Birthday	35
	New Statesman (England)—June	
Robin Fulton:	Mariefred	38
	The Poetry Review (England)—Summer	
Vi Gale:	On the Little North Fork	40
	Poetry Northwest—Spring	
David Greenhood:	To Know a Mountain	42
	Southwest Review—Autumn	
Suzanne Gross:	Lycanthropy	44
	The Beloit Poetry Journal—Spring	
John Gurney:	On Revisiting Keats's Hampstead	47
	New Headland (England)—April	
Robin Hamilton:	Canzone: The Incomplete Amorist	49
	Outposts (England)—Spring	
Robin Hamilton:	Lucifer's Version	51
	Outposts (England)—Winter	
Barbara Harris:	When This Ends, And It Will	53
	The Southern Review—Spring	
Keith Harris:	The Attic	54
	Outposts (England)—Summer	
Anthony Hecht:	After the Rain	55
	The New Yorker—September 9	
David Holbrook:	Birthday Party	57
	Twentieth Century (England)—Vol. CLXXIX, No. 1049	
A. D. Hope:	Parabola	59
	Poetry—August	
Harry Humes:	Autumn's Trout	61
	The Virginia Quarterly Review—Winter	
Harry Humes:	The Muskellunge	63
	The Virginia Quarterly Review—Winter	
Josephine Jacobsen:	The Mexican Peacock	65
	The New Yorker—June 24	

Louis Johnson:	Daughters of Men	66
	New Poetry (Australia)—June	
Maxine Kumin:	Stones	67
	Saturday Review—March 25	
Terry Larsen:	The Black Sun	68
	New Poetry (Australia)—February/April	
Jack Lasenby:	Report to You	71
	Poetry Australia (Australia)—No. 44	
David R. Lenson:	When the Sun Has Died	73
	Quarterly Review of Literature—Vol. XVIII, No. 1–2	
Philip Levine:	Losing You	75
	Poetry—November	
Wes Magee:	Survival Story	77
	Prism International (Canada)—Spring	
Frank Manley:	Lightning Bugs	79
	Partisan Review—#1	
Roger Mitchell:	Poem	80
	The Minnesota Review—Spring	
Ian Mudie:	The Skin	83
	Poetry Australia (Australia)—No. 43	
Leslie Norris:	A Small War	85
	The Anglo-Welsh Review (Wales)—Spring	
Leslie Norris:	Beachmaster	87
	The London Magazine (England)—March	
Leslie Norris:	Bridges	89
	The Atlantic Monthly—June	
Leslie Norris:	Old Voices	90
	The Atlantic Monthly—March	
Harry W. Paige:	A Value of the Absolute	92
	Spirit—Spring/Winter	
John Peck:	Søren	93
	The New Yorker—May 27	
Richard Pevear:	The Beautiful Acceptance	95
	The Hudson Review—Vol. XXIV, No. 4—Winter	
Stanley Plumly:	For J., Ardea Occidentalis	96
	Northwest Review—Vol. XII, No. 1—Fall/Winter	
Al Purdy:	"Old Man Mad About Painting"	97
	Canadian Forum (Canada)—September	

Jarold Ramsey:	Love in an Earthquake	99
	Quarterly Review of Laterature—Vol. XVIII, No. 1–2	
Campbell Reeves:	The Goose-Girl	100
	Southern Poetry Review—Special Issue	
Reg Saner:	Voices at the Edge of the Mirror	102
	Prairie Schooner—Spring	
David Schloss:	A Suicide Pact	103
	Chicago Review—Vol. 24, No. 3—Winter	
Michael Schmidt:	Scorpion	105
	Poetry—February	
Peter Scupham:	Lesson in Survival	107
	Outposts (England)—Spring	
R. E. Sebenthall:	Nativities	108
	Perspective—Winter	
Joan Murray Simpson:	Flying from Dublin	110
	Outposts (England)—Spring	
Ann Stanford:	Down, Down	111
	The Virginia Quarterly Review—Summer	
Peter Steele:	Children's Games	112
	Poetry Australia (Australia)—No. 44	
Edward Storey:	The Dead and the Living	114
	The Critical Quarterly (England)—Spring	
Adrien Stoutenburg:	Cellar	115
	Poetry Northwest—Autumn	
Mark Strand:	Elegy for My Father	117
	Field—Spring	
Jon Swan:	Omen	120
	The New Yorker—September 23	
R. S. Thomas:	The Hand	121
	Poetry Wales (Wales)—Spring	
Charles Tomlinson:	Over Elizabeth Bridge	122
	The London Magazine (England)—April	
Mark Van Doren:	The Possessed	124
	The Hudson Review—Summer	
Ted Walker:	Afterwards	125
	The New Yorker—October 7	
Tom Wayman:	Childermas hymn: December 28, 1970	126
	Canadian Forum (Canada)—January/February	

Theodore Weiss: Before the Night 129
Esquire—September
Nancy G. Westerfield: Reading the Rites 131
Arizona Quarterly—Vol. 27, No. 4—Winter
Jack Zucker: Beginnings 132
Southern Poetry Review—Spring

Best Poems of 1972

ADVENT

That Heaven should be hid is normal. Singular
any part of me should for one instant
be its hiding place. Yet for eight long months I've carried
everything I see and things I shall never see
because I carry Him. At first I scarcely

dared to move; but a shell suffers the whole weight
of the sea and the greenest pod is open
to the thrashing of the wind till the very moment
it is rent, so I trusting walk and grow
heavier with Heaven at every step. I reach

from hill to hill, break out of rocks, enter
flowers and trees and go fourfooted with the beasts
for, until he is strong enough to bear
His weak, new state, I must bear with Him.
How shall I survive the hour Heaven looks up

at me without perhaps any recognition,
demanding still only this hard faith
and the usual needs of a new born child?
Already, the hands that run along this plank
are not wholly mine nor are these feet that cross

and recross the floor. As often as I
replace these dwindling candles with others
tall and white, that cast before me their clean
favouring shadows, I am myself renewed.
I shall always link the sharp smell

of fresh felled wood with this time of waiting
to cradle Him who cradles all the world,
that I already cradle privily
but must bring forth without strife or falsehood
or one concession save those I make to His

own unbelievable abiding self.
Meanwhile, I eat and sleep and sometimes laugh
at my own partridge shape nothing can now disguise
and at the cock's abrupt and dazzling cry
weep for a nameless fear as women will.

NOEL WELCH

IN THE FACE OF DESCENT

1
She said

   My God, he's falling.

I watched the whole thing in her face:
   her eyes descending with him,
   her mouth sprung open,
   a ventriloquist's hole.

The sound when he reached earth
   was of distant dynamiting.

She put one hand across her mouth and nose
   as if someone had grabbed her from behind.

I could not turn away from her.
All I said was

   Is he dead?

2
Afterwards I might have said:

there was something in the ragged pitch of clouds—

the shadows slanted too abruptly to the lawn—

I was too calm.

But always after the fact.
Better not to be clairvoyant
   as she was
if only because the suffering stretches out.

Her back to me at dawn
and curtains blowing to her face
she said

    Something is wrong today.

My bitter laugh was for love
    dying night by night,
    guttering in vacant motions of our bodies.

Her face closed over my laughter all morning.

3

I think his father said he was fifteen
    and had been climbing flagpoles
    since he was eight.
The old man had arthritis
and was reduced to handling ropes
from below.

An ordinary face:
    pale, a little acned—
    and he stood as though
    the big bones of his hands
    were hard to lift.

But when she said

    You're young to go so high

it was the smile that tipped him
favorably into light
as though he had a vantage point
from poles that we would never know.

He said

    I'm old enough.

Odd to hear a human being
    say only one thing in his lifetime.

He did not even cry out when he fell.

4

It was sixty feet tall.

I said

    why do you want to watch if
    you're only going to worry?

She would not give me more than

    We're paying for it, aren't we?

I came and went twice.
Still she was there,
her arms folded
watching the way the father stood below
and sent up what the boy needed.

I threw rocks in the lake
    wanting to break through the surface of her face,
    fall and plunge as we used to
    when to come into her was

    to bring back things I valued
    all day long.

She said

    My God, he's falling.

5

His father's back was turned.
Neither of us saw him fall.
Only my wife.

The spine snapped.
  He landed precisely
    on the back of his neck
    and all his weight
    followed down on it
    as though his own body
    fell across his shoulders

We did not fly the flag that summer
or walk on the point
or accept the crying of curlews.

Her face is now
the face of all things descending
and in her eyes
I watch them falling.

        T. ALAN BROUGHTON

SEVEN PRELUDES TO SILENCE

1

All day a wounded mountain followed me,
gentle and crumpled like a fern.
It was too shy to speak of its great need
and what could I have done to help it?

2

The desert has forgotten what it is waiting for.
Even sand will not survive without a purpose.
Can dust learn to swim? Will flowers
be able to repeat themselves in stone?

3

We have removed the earth's flesh and torn out
its bleeding veins. Sunlight reflects
from our knives. It blisters the surface
of the lake where nebulae of fish will never
return. A few gulls carry their white grief
on delicate hollow bones from water to water.

4

We have forgotten that once there were black
swans with brilliant red beaks and curly
tail feathers. Soon the last birds of desperate
passage will ricochet through our oily rooms.

5

The stars confirm nothing, deny nothing. Heads
of animals grow on our walls. Their hopeless
glass eyes stare down at us without reproach.

6
We who invented the clock and the metronome
cannot keep the calendar alive. We exist,
not on the edge of life but at its limits,
asking no pardon of the grass or the empty
shells which arrive and depart on each tide.

7
In the book of our history it will be recorded
that we murdered the earth. With the name
of a different crime tattooed on each finger
we walk out into the orchard and find
tiny mirrors hanging from the trees. Listen.
The leaves are screaming for help as they fall.

RICHARD SHELTON

WASSAIL

for R. T.

Neath, Glamorgan., South Wales
Christmas Eve 1964

I scrape the ice from Auntie's bedroom window.
The sea wind tunes its air bells for rough weather.
In Skewen, you are asleep and the winter man
comes from the hill, marking the frozen houses
for life or death. All over Wales and England,
Father Christmas gets up in his threadbare
dressing gown. In your Mother's kitchen, the turkey
carcass pokes its blunt legs at the cold wall.
The peas and sprouts lie tenderly in water,
the Marks' and Spencer's cake, the Turkish Delight,
wait in the green tree's eye, the coals' light loving
ten-dimensional photographs enshrined on the hearth ledge.

    You will pass through
    this singular assault.
    All evil is not what it seems.
    It is the more difficult choice
    to create an alienation.

I am having tea downstairs,
and rum and gin and Irish stout
and bloody ovaltine.

    The house has no
    equilibrium.

    There is a ghost.

In Swansea this morning, the Christmas flowers
flew out of their buckets of ice water
dancing a turbine of red
over the cardboard Christchild.

I had a vision of fat Dylan
stumbling down a corridor
of seawater to Laugharne
leering at the little eels.

By Manorbier we climbed so high
above the sea that emerald
and blue swam up to drown loud birds.

Dark time of Pleiades. The gale
feeds brutal autumn to Sirius.

Houses on Arthur Street purse their doors.
The last bus to Cimla grinds black sleet.

We are buried in phenomena.
We cannot touch.
The winter man will come to our last sleep,
where the gulls fall in thorns of grass
    and the great horn of ice
pours no sound through the wind to call us home.

KAYWYNNE ADAMS

AFTER DEATH

Opening up the house
After three weeks away
I found bird droppings
All over the ground floor,
White and heavy on the windows,
On the worktop,
On the cupboards,
On every wild hope of freedom.

I could not find any bird
At first, and feared
Some science fiction mystery,
To be horribly explained
As soon as whatever
It was felt sure
It had got me alone,
A mile from the village.

At last I discovered him,
Weightless and out of the running,
More null than old wrapping paper
A month after Christmas.
No food inside him of course,
He had died of hunger
And no waste either,
He was quite empty.

His desperate ghost
Flew down my throat and my ears.
There was no air
He had not suffered in.
He lay in one place,
His droppings were everywhere
More vivid, more terrible
Than he had been, ever.

PATRICIA BEER

SOCRATES

When Socrates found Socrates in hell,
it did not strike those men as at all strange
that they should wander thus and thus exchange
ideas with one another, and looks as well.
"This is the way it is," said one of them,
"when a man spends his life in irony,
his mind like two flowers on a single stem,
death but reflects him, he is never free
of his image, which is truer for having died."
"That's true enough," he replied.

"I have now learned that there is no such thing
as thought in company, though I knew it then"—
he looked hard at that other pug-nosed man—
"I say I knew it even while bantering
truth into patency among my friends;
I knew I'd made them what they are, that they
were only mirrors to myself, loose ends
of my stranded thinking, now tucked away.
They could not free themselves, although they tried."
"That's true enough," he replied.

"There is no end of thinking, and no end,
for one who has begun, of being alone.
Perhaps in war or politics or the stone-
encircled priesthood one might have a friend,
but not in thinking. That the ancient gods
are always misconceived, that poetry
lies in its teeth, and that it makes no odds
whether one fails or flourishes, being free:
all this I knew, and had nothing, and died."
"That's true enough," he replied.

BENJAMIN K. BENNETT

AFTER WALKING TO & FRO
& UP & DOWN IN IT

the kitchen is sleeping.
there aren't any motorcycles
sneering in machine gun thunder
up the hill outside the window,
only two tiny lungs
quivering like tattered
new year's eve crepe.

in the refrigerator bottles of beer
graze like bison on the Great Plains,
lamplight shines thru the toes
of my groaning feet. bones
are cracked pottery—bathtubs
are saviors.

my thoughts are still in hand-to-hand
combat with reflex, an
indigestion of the present.
I will graze awhile with the bison
& swim with the saviors
then slip my cancelled eyes into
the slot marked sleep putting
in my request for a brand new pair.

the night will be as peaceful
as a deserted battleship while death
out in the hills digs a hole,
its shovel striking rocks
ringing like a telephone, the grave
is a wrong number
that we answer anyway.

Douglas Blazek

GRAND PAUSE

How did you die so soon? I only held you,
And in your eightfold kiss read prophecy,
When dolphins foamed and rode before the wake
And thunderheads broke open in your cry

A junction much more strange than earth and joy,
A marriage as impossible as fish and weather.
Surface, love, and breathe, for nature's sake!
Where you bask now, we cannot swim together.

O conches! There you ride, borne on the deep.
How did I fail to know you would go down?
Hands' oars, sails' breath, the body's barque
Blow out to sea across the combers of your sleep,
Where rain can never rain, nor old moon frown,
Nor lover see the roses of the land grow dark.

JAMES BLISH

WEAR

I hate how things wear out.

Not elbows, collars, cuffs;
they fit me, lightly frayed.

Not belts or paint or rust,
not routine maintenance.

On my own hook I cope
with surfaces: with all

that rubs away, flakes off, or fades
on schedule. What eats at me

is what wears from the in-
side out: bearings, couplings,

universal joints, old
differentials, rings,

and points: frictions hidden
in such dark they build

to heat before they come
to light. What gets to me

is how valves wear, the slow
leak in old circuitry,

the hairline fracture under
stress. With all my heart

I hate pumps losing prime,
immeasurable over—

loads, ungauged fatigue
in linkages. I hate

myself for wasting time
on hate: the cost of speed

came with the bill of sale;
the rest was never under

warranty. Five years
ago I turned-in every

year; this year I rebuild
rebuilt parts. What hurts

is how blind tired I get.

        PHILIP BOOTH

BUILDING A TERRACE

Sentimental nonsense of course to talk
Of the "living rock" or the "honesty" of stone—
But the words are in my mind each time I dig
Some stubborn chunk of sandstone out of the earth,
Split, dress and settle it into place
In wall or terrace; and I think of two dead men:
My grandfather Will Rogers, and Archimedes.
"Give me a lever," he said, "and I'll shift the world."
Rocks that a man can't lift can smash a foot—
And when, after crowbar, shovel and mattock have done
Their work, you feel a big stone gently tilt
And shift at a sweating finger's touch you know
In your bones what the old Greek meant. Archimedes
May have been just a name to Grandad, but
He loved stone and worked it till he died.
Seventy-five he was and stood as straight
As when he'd landed thirty years before
With his box of tools, his family and his lodge
Certificate: Oddfellows Master at Bridgnorth
In Shropshire—*Amicitia, amor
Et veritas* beneath the eye of God.
In Sydney it meant nothing. But he worked:
Anonymous flagged paths, hearths, terraces,
Fireplaces that draw and walls that stand
Are his memorial. He whistled, sang,
Was gentle, smelled of mortar, sawdust, sweat
And the open air. "Drunk again," he'd say,
Laughing under old-fashioned moustaches when
I fell running to watch him split the stone.
He was an artist—he could knock a tune
Out of an old tin can, they said—and when
His sledge-hammer rang on his steel wedges the rock
Broke clean and straight. I touched the fresh
Rock-faces that had never seen the sun.
At home, he said, sinking a well they found

A frog alive inside a hollow rock
Ten feet beneath the ground. He built a wall
The day before he died—surprised by death
Like that old man in Syracuse who fell
Under the ignorant Roman soldier's spear
Face down across his drawings in the sand.

                R. F. Brissenden

THE USHERS

Rain in the pines. Cross-rhythms of rain,
long and short interweaving. Locky, the bitch pup,
part shepherd, part mongrel, named for her being
so beautifully locked in and up,
snug head and heart and loins
like a thicket hiding a bird, ranges
away and away from me,
parabolas of curiosity,
cross-rhythms searching, here, there, in, out,
the pine trees' secrets;
these pines, red pines, half-grown in rainlight,
a twenty-year-old grove that somebody set
in the lines of his vision. His name was Davis.
He was, I judge, an orderly man and planted
his trees in rank and file, so leaving

a place of many avenues where I saunter
in slow imagination under hazy crowns
that glow with rainwater,
aquamarine.
The rain rhythms are almost words, whispers
in moist light, and the pines are ushers
that lead me down these lanes, their boughs
on either side gesturing, bending low,
sweeping me onward, while Locky runs free
among the avenues.
What secret, girl? Mouse lair? Squirrel tree?
Sweet forms of pregnant snowshoe hare? Whose
woods are these, really? She returns, snuffling zigzag,
looks at me, her brow creased, one foot lifted, then goes,
a secret. The pines bow to me, the lines beg

for my attention, touching my elbows,
ushering me on toward . . . toward what? Dimness
is a part of the pine grove,
the comforting rain darkness,
and squirrel-shriek is a part, the floor sown
with fragrant brown damp needles like shreds of tobacco
is a part, the friendliest part, resilient,
giving nudge for nudge to my footprints;
whispering is a part. And my hipbone, is it
a part?——that I treated like dirt
for forty years, never knew, needed, missed,
until now, in rain and pines, its pain is my support.
Arthritis is normal, an aspect of aging, everyone
has it who lives long enough, if that's a comfort.
Everyone except the pines. They lead me on.

This place belongs to the pines whose needles
filter such acid into the earth that nothing else
grows here, except the interlopers,
Locky and me and the false
beechdrops ringing soundless bells, the amanitas
springing in bloodless dance. This place
belongs to the pines and the pines belong
to whom? Leading, guiding me on,
solicitous, their drooping limbs on either side.
This way, this way, come . . .
But look, where the grove thins out, ahead,
look at the light there, glowing in the open,
suddenly brilliant, golden, touched with rose,
shimmering above steeplebush. And listen.
Why do I hear nothing? Whose

are these woods? When did the whispering stop?
Was it rain or pines? What is that light?
Locky, where are you? Come, good dog, good dog.
Why is that light so bright?
Something tells me something. Let go, you god
damned pines. Must I be led? Drop
your wet limbs off me.
Eh, have you found it, Locky,
there where we buried it? Why would they lead us
from this peace? Thrusting
me on to the edge where steeplebush
encroaches and the orderly lines grow thin
and light shimers. Locky, Locky, where are you?
Come here, come, I never buried anything.
Something has crossed me. I am going through.

HAYDEN CARRUTH

THE HEIR

How we prepared for you. Nights
carefully, we would climb
into the long darkness
where you were lurking
made for you new
arms and head and
small new body to begin again in.
Nights out of our love for each other
we made you that small body.
We created it, meticulous, patiently.
How we were God making it.
It was perfect. A house. A safe
house to be at ease in.

Clasped on the verge
of the desert where you walk
how we called out your name
that we were ready.
We called out your name
where you were withered and poison
in the shredded dark.

From the edge, the brink
you watch us without eyes.
The softness of bodies
the warm house we have prepared for you.
You would leap across the darkness
but you have no body.
You would weep
but you have no voice.
You would cry out to us to
come
and find you, but we can't hear.
You watch us call you without eyes.
O here there is no way in.
Here is all flesh and hard bone.
Child.
They are pouring bandages on your
broken house.

JENI COUZYN

RETURN

Well, I've come back to the place where your bones are,
bringing your children, pigtailed, almost reading.
My eyes ache.
You would think, you would think,
after five years.... But the reddish clay
is still like blood.
                    We have Christmas together,
your family and I. They do not speak of you,
as if I were here for some other reason—

> *I cower in this vaulted*
> *silence, but the stabbing light might—*

yet they must grieve in their way.
They grieve. Each ornament on the tree
is their memory, for the children.

> *There are too many of them,*
> *all these people who are not*
> *you, but have your hair, your eyes,*
> *your speech, energy, some of your ways;*
> *the arched sky crashes, splinters,*
>   *as to stars   to celebrate a child's*
>   *birth here—*

But, in the dark, the cut tree looms, its
electric eyes transfix me, and its gaudy
claws surround, clutch. I say,
"How lovely!" lying (our daughters watch),
sleep, sleep. The Yule tides rise

> *I drown, my fists*
> *full of wet stones.*

                              PATRICIA CUMMING

CLOUDS

The clouds moved in another hundred feet
during the night, just as they have done
each night for the past two weeks.
Now they hang barely beyond the range
of thrown stones. The sun is someone else's story,
the rich relation of a slight acquaintance.

Bending over us, the clouds have the texture
of faces seen through smoke.
Thoughts in a confused mind look like that.
Tell me again that they are not hostile,
that they have come merely out of curiosity
to see again if we are possible.

If so, then why are doors more difficult to open
as if some sadness were leaning against them?
Why do windows darken and trees bend
when there is no wind? You call that occasional
roar the roar of a plane and I imagine
a time when I might have believed that.

But now the darkness has been going on
for too long, and I have accustomed myself
to the pleasure of thinking that soon
there will be no reason to hold on in this place
where rocks are like water and it's so difficult
to find something solid to hold on to.

STEPHEN DOBYNS

STILLBORN

Not to be is to be.

When memory like an inverted waterfall
Pours back the past upon us
And only long grieving links the hours together
We lie awake in utter loneliness,
Half-listening for a cry that can not come
From the antique cradle occupied by others
Where others heard the small thin sound
From that source which forevermore for us is silent.

When we begin again that wracking effort
To bring the lost into being, all that once
Was rapture ends now in withdrawal,
In pain. The trauma of the womb
Of life which bore that death
Afflicts us both. We dare not try again
To conceive another lest the ghost
Of one nonliving who haunts
Our minds and hearts unbearably
Haunt another being, born, along his life forever.

We turn, through empty midnights, toward each other
For consolation. But there is no consolation.
We dredge the long deep distances of time
To draw back into this room
One from nowhere who was already here,
Borne by the grief of two beings in a blind bed,
A soft body between us.

And the act that would begin others ends for us,
Becomes in our sick minds a profanation.
In nearness of sorrow all seems incestuous.

There was one who came from me and entered you,
And was issued forth into a nonexistence,
Uninheritor of our doom,
On whom no hurt of life nor its final
Fatality could ever have fallen.

Let us clasp now this deathless child,
With all our love, between us
While the quick clock goes ticking out our own
Midnight with no morning, until neverbeing
Becomes one with everbeing.

Not to be is to be.

Carleton Drewry

THE CHILDREN

The problem is more and more
in the eyes   how to understand
the beautiful issue
of children moving on the earth

as the old masters did
when they painted children
and virgins   their faces
are all newly fleshed   the eyes
barely settled in

as if coming into this new dimension
each cell of their bodies
turned its opposite side.

The problem is more and more
in the mind   how to see
the mystery of children
as they move into their spaces

with the old wisdom   now gone
that a child grew
in the eye of each rose
there is nothing
left to know.

The problem is more and more
what is not understood:
the astral loveliness singing in their blood

the light at the soft
blurred edges of the moon
collecting in luminous circles
around the eyes of infants.

Harley Elliott

THE COAT

After so many years,
standing with me in the same mirror,
it is almost transparent.
In the morning I rise up and enter it—
this skin frayed at the wristbones, this suitcase
of old weathers, slick with shine, sagging
with the weight of inner pockets.

At night I slide it off, and the darkness
slides into it, slips its fingers inside,
and touches what the day has left:
old bills, dry webs of hair, salt,
a leaf thin and sharp as a bird's thigh.
What do I care what the dark does,
rifling my coat like an old wife?

Throw it on a stool to beg,
dance with it the long nights,
fold it after the funeral—what do I care?
When I lie down naked to sleep
it wears my own slouch.
I breathe in. Breathe out.
In a dark corner, it fills.

PETER EVERWINE

ORESTES

for George Seferis

On the track on the track once more the breathless track
the fast banked turns where the names of stallions float
and the axles whir in the wind and the eyes look on
and sing his praises high in the victor's car
he lifts his arms to the crowd and the sun comes over
the sea that gave him life and gives him glory now

this daybreak how many daybreaks more on the track
the murderous turns where the stallions strain for air
and the axles heat under foot your knees are buckling
yes and conscience cries you on it lashes you on
and the mother sea is lost and the sun blacks out
and thunder rolling thunder drums you far from home

down rockfalls how many rockfalls more on the track
the crucial turns where the breakneck stallions plunge
and the axles screech in flames and the furies race
my heart beats faster headlong on on I can see
the great gods laughing on the heights the acropolis
look the impossible sunrise blazing dead ahead

ROBERT FAGLES

HIGH TORQUE

The fast getaway
at the gold light....
Output multiplied
past self-performance
Force applied
to a terse wheel-turn
of distance   Clean
pick-up in slogs
of traffic thickened
as sloughs   Twist
of an expert wind-
at-my-heels I have
to fly before   Quick,
be arcane, cunning,
drive-shaft wringing
a rear pursuit
Manoeuver me clear
of despond   Be me
but merlin-motor
more   O I'll
leap forward openly
as roads permit
an engine magnified
Move me   Me *move!*

Norma Farber

LOOKING AT THE COELACANTH

For some fish, I tell myself,
extinction's harder than survival.
For sheer indestructibility
I take the sermon of old fourlegs,
coeval with dodo, dinosaur, saber-toothed tiger.

For all his fossil leavings
unearthed from Greenland to Ohio,
in Madagascar, Bavaria, even New Jersey
at the base of the Princeton Library—
for all his pre-trilobite fixtures

finally mounted in museum cages:
primal as ever, the very fellow intact swims free
in his fathoms of Indian Ocean,
pompous with fins set into peduncles
like circus-dwarf limbs gaited to convulse the gallery.

I could learn by looking
into the chrysolite poignance of his clown-eye.
Under the rise and fall of suns,
in my parvenu trembling of species,
I embrace him: perdurable cousin of my ancestor.

Stubborn funnyman, stay me against my time.

NORMA FARBER

THEORY OF FLIGHT

That beginning, those few yards over and above ground,
how the running beast gliding amazed himself
to be somehow streaking only half

touching his planet, not even half grabbing
Jurassic surfaces in an initial spurt
of striding-in-air, starting

wildly anew, wings pumping for dear
transitional life. Who did he think he was,
the precursor, with his dull unfunctional feathers, claws

horn-sheathed for earthbound stalking?
He felt a fool, God's own clown calling
attention to unlikely saltation. Watch him fall!

the woods hooted. Sharp-toothed cousins
grinned clamping his long reptilian tail.
He dug something like a human fingernail

in the mud to wrench up beyond muck
and mutilation, launching ponderously. He could have burst
with the scrape and fumble of being first

to try what he'd never in a hundred million years
have pinion enough to perfect.... Anyway, praise
to his take-off from his kind, still cackling in ooze.

NORMA FARBER

ON HIS SIXTIETH BIRTHDAY
11 . ii . 1972

Fathers must tell their children of injustice
And cruelty, between the rewarding toil
Of lessons on the bassethorn and readings
Aloud of Arthur Conan Doyle.

It may be thought life's sense, if sense at all,
Comes in the minor artists' artifact:
The variations on minute perceptions
Heroically destined for neglect;

That anguished harmony, those chiming stanzas —
Of twigs and whiskers the painstaking scribes —
Left for improbable future recognition
Like girls grown up from storm-entrusted babes.

Curious that the robin was observed
By villein, monarch, merchant, factory-hand.
But if you look behind you to the fork,
Oblique in the garden, my particular friend

(Warily glancing back on straddled pins)
Is thickly white along his foggy wings.
There are as many different birds as poets;
One bird despite man's botched imaginings.

Wrong, wrong to say that February is mild,
And equally that February is severe.
In age we come to welcome February
For what he is, of arbitrary power.

The stares' preliminary coughing: will
Fate let me see them through to actual lieder?
No matter, since already tiny green
Arches have gothicized the frosty border.

Yet, glimpsed below disordered grasses, man's
Muddled footfalls printed in the mud
Remind us awesomely that still to come
Is the atrocious murder of the god.

So often art's devices are naïve:
That watchman's horn after the fugal flurry
Sounding again, a true goodnight; the axe
Struck in the flies on anything but cherry —

Paralleled by the care of man for men:
Such private trouble as is taken by
Schoolmaster referees and wholesome nurses —
The other love that makes us want to cry.

Now oceanographers believe that oceans
Are transient, that even Asias move
Around, like sandwiches, on rocky salvers.
Thus the green swellings of the globe may prove

To mask fatalities worse than they engender.
What wonder then that human life's a mess,
Its very scenery not yet arranged
To satisfy the director's finickiness.

And can the state of art surprise us when
We think of the condition of the State —
Although expecting that the artist's weakness
Will somehow make mankind inviolate?

So, sneezing in this cold bare kingdom, one
Dreams wildly: yes, I may be there for Spring —
Meaning, say, for the end of cruelty,
Meaning the subsequent great leap's beginning.

And finally one almost comes to feel
Sorry for February, its melancholy
Austerity so threatened by renewal.
Threatened, one says, but knowing that the tree

Can't help the shuddering rising of the sap,
Descent of blushing tassels, sparkling stars —
That even now one's faith makes out in those
Nailed branches black against the sunset's bars.

Roy Fuller

MARIEFRED

for Ella and Östen Sjöstrand

1
the mists are not quite down on the shorn field

the ghosts are not yet rustling with old age
but stand around me calmly, apple-trees
sun-flowers, all stooped and ripening still

autumn has never haunted me with such wealth
as now: isn't it time to believe the ghosts at last
my feelings simple as maple leaves with crimson veins
my thoughts a generous confusion?

the mists are not quite down on the shorn field
where a reaping-machine waits, beyond harvest,
a long neck a jawbone too rigid to droop

2
in the silence
in the white light:
yellowing oaks
the lake still blue and free
no line of vision blocked

neither flaw nor darkness in the crystal wall

my knowledge is:
acid in the soil
the weight of fruit pulling to its own decay

in the silence
in the white light:
a branch of cherries

my knowledge is too clear
I look straight through as if it weren't there

3

not a ghost but a clear warning:
survival, as the white of a birch bole survives
the rust of autumn

the mind is a silver landscape—one breath
will mist over a lifetime's knowledge:
in the landscape beyond the clear windows
—wastage of seed

the lanes between the red wooden houses
lead me through both landscapes
my breath white in the air

and I too am now one of the ghosts:
we know the warnings, we know—they survive
generation upon generation

                                  ROBIN FULTON

ON THE LITTLE NORTH FORK

My favorite dream. We are camped
 in lodgepole pine, in a clearing
  along the North Fork.

Newly married, we have sweated
 an old DeSoto over back roads
  from pump to repair shop to water.

The borrowed tent looks leaky,
 smells of mildew and stale tar.
  We don't sneeze, we are drunk

on wild white syringa
 headier than orange or jasmine.
  We've caught, cleaned and cooked

a late dinner. Last chores—
 you're weighting the tarp, turning down
  the Coleman, coming in to bed.

In this dream we haven't stood
 at family biers, quarreled over
  money. We haven't fretted

in hospital solariums, dreaded
 X-ray and serology reports
  or met up with cantankerous

landlords. We know nothing about
 mortgages, closing costs. Loan sharks
  are pulp novel denizens.

The war is six months old.
 For us, two weeks away, remote
  as headlines, old soldiers

or uncles in bonus marches.
    Diuretics and wonder drugs
        are for hypochrondriacs.

We haven't been unfaithful,
    each in his fashion, or
        faithful. We do not know

our true selves. We steer by the closest
    star, a double rainbow,
        know what we sense precisely

in the moment's blown bubble.
    Sweet saving dream, flower-sprigged
        as that early meadow in pine,

like our awakening, our aging,
    it depends on a dark underside
        of troubled anchoring roots.

Vi Gale

TO KNOW A MOUNTAIN

That earthen noble
  stout   mutable   gruff
that delicate nuancer of sun
  the knowable mountain

One must heed sun
  to know a mountain
heed the hateless strife going on
undream the dreamed-in deities
  redundant in its darknesses
foretell back
  what it is that happens

To foretell pastward the events
  that are a mountain
is to act within
  in one's own way
  even as a mountain
    has acted within
    in a mountain's own way
    each time forth
    with its selfhood

To envision this tumult of rock
  with this turbulence of sun-made air
    each changing by invading the other
is to witness a becoming
  that is a perishing
    a failing that is a forming

To act within
   to replay what has been happening
      within a mountain and without
         from when it was no mountain
            only a future word
               for what was before oneself was
is to worship by knowing

When one knows how to know it
   a mountain moves—
      it comes to one.

                              DAVID GREENHOOD

LYCANTHROPY

I am old suddenly, overnight:
not as a man may live long and grow
old but as an animal is old
if it survives to reach a human's
years of youth. My face, that men must judge
me by, is changed: roughly hooded with
shaggy hair grizzled to the eyebrows;
and my eyes in any company
I know glitter with danger, not now
what I threaten but what threatens me.

I too have noticed how my teeth are
broken and displaced to writhe my lips
in a voiceless grimace of distrust.
I can see that, and the long jawbone
thrusting out the muzzle of my face
to find in invisible shiftings
of air the secrets I must master.
I see it well enough: that my face
is the face of an old wolf that was

alpha wolf even in earliest
maturity, the terror and teacher
of the running deer, and the nightmare
bogey of apathetic shepherds
and complacent sheep; stark defender
and preserver of my own, fearless
and fierce, and exasperating men
with an intelligence they hated
to have to acknowledge. When even
strangers see my face they see in it
I am deposed; those who were my friends

can see there how I have no friends, how
any that goes with me goes by chance
or by necessity, and never
for long; and how since I am driven
to, I choose to be solitary,
secret as the snow: a track, a voice,

a shadow at the farthest edges
of my former range; and so I seem
mysterious, and so more cunning
and more deadly than I ever was.

I am trap and rifle wise, I know,
none wiser in a land where I am
prey. In any mirror, even ice,
I see how old and new suspicions
mold my face with hunger: all structures
are to trap me and all sticks to kill:
all that man may make is for my harm.

Such sleep as I dare indulge in now
is haunted by the ache of loping
endlessly along the path that bounds
my only home, that line within which
I am outcast, a mere intruder
beyond. Now it is always winter

in my dreams, snow over everything,
even the trees, a high, white, tiny
moon freezing the opened earth and sky.
Everywhere the streams are frozen deep;
I run on meandering rivers
of ice, perfectly silent, alone,
knowing all the time it is a dream,
but whether of the past or future
or of something I myself desire,
I do not know. Sometimes, forgetting,
or weakened by hope, I lift my head

to send a sorrowing chill music
arcing outward from my clouded mouth.
Men say that a wolf howls; my people
call it song. Never, almost never
will a distant singer of my kind
respond, and if one does at last, we
make a moving chord of loneliness
a while, and then sink back to silence,
never meeting and afraid to meet.

SUZANNE GROSS

ON REVISITING KEATS'S HAMPSTEAD

All's long performed, the lungs returned to fire,
the walls and floors scraped clean of their disease,
the doors and windows ashes in a pyre,
casts taken of the four extremities;
the body laid beneath its broken lyre,
dawn buried, with its Greek obituaries,
the last unopened letters by the corpse
as annotation, or as afterthought.

You diagnosed your end, read every vowel
coughed up among the debris of your breath
while vomiting your stomach by the bowl,
your pulse vibrating like an aspen leaf;
held down the brain, controlled the broken soul
with all the ambiguities of death;
tormented, as your virgin memory passed
haphazard facts of passion in the grass.

How could you know what promises concerned
the nightingale's decision and device,
what womanhood was skulking in the bird
or maenad waited in the angel's voice,
what interrupted lust lay in the urn
and held the heifer down in sacrifice:
what isolation took its Autumn way
without a glance towards the poet's eye. . ?

All long since over, and the third room's closed.
Some fourth perhaps is opened, where the sport
hereditary dispenses as it blows
is brought back to the balancing of thought
defining feeling, bringing back the rose
from its corrupt descending into nought;
explaining, in some place of mystery,
there is no place for final tragedy.

I watch you like a picture, half-asleep
withdrawn and self-existent in a chair,
your will away in moonlight, as it weeps
its bodies featured from the gods' stray tears,
your blood run from the bone, the fissure deep,
your life carved like a statuary of fear
some figment of illusion, worth a frown,
like things the living finger, then put down.

For you had seen as gods, had realised
the purpose of affliction in the way
that suffering takes the soul, that hourly dies
into a broken strangeness, as the day's
old long-forgotten motives, re-arise
and spell the first death of identity.
Best draw the veil, withdraw the memory
of one who looked too deeply in the sea.

Yet this remains, the room that held your breath,
the chair you sat in by the window frame
that gave out on the garden, then the heath;
the bird within the plumtree, as it flamed
each visionary cliche into death;
all relics now, as dead as carnal pain.
I walk, disdaining sorrow, play my part;
the classical detachment of the heart. . .

JOHN GURNEY

CANZONE: THE INCOMPLETE AMORIST

for the Italians of the dolce stil nuovo

1

We are defined by a limited repertoire of gestures:
The hand that stroked Helen's cheek
Makes the same movement as it touches
Chlöe's breast. Nor can we command much variety
In our argument: the words once said
Must be repeated at each new encounter.
And so our skill increases in facility
But muzzles the response in ritual gestures,
To one phrase, I love you; passion in chains:
The actor dies, as we observe his acts.

2

As well perhaps; for thus our ways become
The colour-codes of dangerous areas,
Inadequately traversed. Crossing the river,
We build the bridge that we must use again;
Other rivers are crossed by that same bridge:
From heart to heart it stretches out, and if
One or other bank be absent, yet still
It must be built. With these constructed paths
We walk on, to live we must forget
That still the map is not the country.

3

I had watered the dream-flower that grows
In the heart, but found the flourish evanescent
And the fruits not there to pick. Willingly
I would not grow such purple flowers
Within my breast. I cultivate my garden
In the senses, do not need some subtle thought
To charm my pulse to sleep. Rather a
Prophylactic meeting in the night. This
Is not the antique courtesy, but the old
Desire of Adam in my bones.

4

Or so I said; but when I turned to see you
Was it the darkness in my eyes hid you from me?
I could not see my lover for my love.
And so you looked and saw, and came and went,
But what I might have seen had I looked
In another way than my accustomed one,
If I had made a gesture not made before
Or used a word no longer in my lexicon:
We met, and loved, and parted, as travellers
Passing on opposite sides of a bridge.

5

I have had my time, and now cannot return;
The old things have been said, and are done;
The sweet new style is old, and broken out
At the elbow. I would not write "Repentance"
In the book, so turn the pages backwards
Till the end, to come upon the dedication
Where I once began, "To her who taught me
Love loves not the mind," and there rewrite:
The mind divorced from love, breaks down a bridge
That broken once, you never can cross over.

ROBIN HAMILTON

LUCIFER'S VERSION

Eve ate the apple, but ignored the worm;
Explicat, I was there, "Your reporter,"
Detached and superior, an interested party.
Adam condoned the sin, but ignored the context —
I being still there, thought somewhat
Chastened by experience, I had denied
Responsibility, but the excuse did not
Pass current, and out we all
Went, being three rogues together, or
Adam and Eve and the Gentleman.

For a little time, being the proprietor
Of a Punch-and-Judy Show, I relished the
Phrase, Each man a hero in his own epic.

Observing with acclaim the morality
"Play of Cain and Abel," Cain "gaining"
An Oscar, and the Mayoralty of the
City of Babel-under-Sodom, I applied as
"Public Relations Manager and Business Consultant
(Having some experience of evictions)."

My activities became multifarious: in
The lapse between word and deed I
Inserted myself. Rationality became
My watchword. I
Did not so much deceive as distract:
Essential issues became blurred and
In the scope for accommodation,
That accommodation devoured the intent.

Such vague generalities I stocked against
The cold — my tail and tusks became
Notorious, but the frock coat I
Brought out of Eden still concealed
(Though unsympathetically referred to
By One as "A
Whited Sepulchre.")

Deliberately I still regard the times:
Now in a penthouse suite and not the
Boiler basement (Stoking fires in the hot
Ground/ I fought the Lord, and the Lord
Won) I cultivate rumours of my imminent
Defection — The Grand Old Man and His
Thrombosis encourage the derelictions
Of my juniors. Life is pleasant, as
I watch with interest for the Second
Coming of the Flood.

ROBIN HAMILTON

WHEN THIS ENDS, AND IT WILL

And I forget to hold your lovely face
Up to my eyes
What world will curve inside me
To the center where my shell sings?

If I don't hear the green force
Of your words
Or smell your fathers on a wind
The sea blew up from Africa

I will lie like sand
The empty beach
Where waves unwrap
My hair.

No matter, No matter
That your prow
Beached this strange shore.
I cannot say the name.

Far from mother island,
Sister's smile, you are the unholy
Love that sounds
About my ears.

I will sleep and wake one day
To oars that cleave you from me.
God and the world
Go with you.

                      BARBARA HARRIS

THE ATTIC

Delving in realms of familiar junk,
Things concealed yesterday, today revealed,
Tomorrow to cry Eureka for, then hastily dry.
Here dwells Time; opens a store,
Deals in tears by the bucketful,
Lies by the score.

Among humiliating cages, dressmakers' dummies,
Things that go cuckoo when the wind squeaks its shutters,
With tarnished coin we haggle and bargain,
Reflections in a mirror that looks back on everything,
Weigh an old future against a new past.

He will weigh it, will tip the scales,
The columns of figures are years to our credit,
Altruistic natures he'll take into account.
No clock steals a march on Time.

Here our cases of conscience stand
Already packed as though for a journey,
Tied with string that died in its own knot.
He'll have them opened, examined, despatched
From where, stored, with the Christmas decorations,
Because of rising damp, we fret for their safety.

Lonely darkness, cloth of coldness,
He will take it, smooth and fold it,
Fabricate it into a story, stretch it,
Pleat and stitch it into nightwear,
Make us wear it inside out.

Thus we sort memories from things forgotten,
Multiferous things which for long amused us,
Rattle the red dice in the ribbed cup.
Until at last the final throw — the corpse resplendent.

Keith Harris

AFTER THE RAIN

The barbed-wire fences rust
As their cedar uprights blacken
After a night of rain.
Some early, innocent lust
Gets me outdoors to smell
The teasel, the pelted bracken,
The cold, mossed-over well,
Rank with its iron chain,

And takes me off for a stroll.
Wetness has taken over.
From drain and creeper twine,
It's runnelled and trenched and edged
A pebbled serpentine,
Secretly, as though pledged
To attain a difficult goal
And join some important river.

The air is a smear of ashes
With a cool taste of coins.
Stiff among misty washes,
The trees are as black as wicks,
Silent, detached, and old.
A pallor undermines
Some damp and swollen sticks.
The woods are rich with mold.

How even and pure this light!
All things stand on their own,
Equal and shadowless,
In a world gone pale and neuter,
Yet riddled with fresh delight.
The heart of every stone
Conceals a toad, and the grass
Shines with a dowse of pewter.

Somewhere a branch rustles
With the life of squirrels or birds,
Some life that is quick and right.
This queer, delicious bareness,
This plain, uniform light,
In which both elms and thistles,
Grass, boulders, even words
Speak for a Spartan fairness,

Might, as I think it over,
Speak in a form of signs,
If only one could know
All of its hidden tricks,
Saying that I must go
With a cool taste of coins,
To join some important river,
Some damp and swollen Styx.

Yet what puzzles me the most
Is my unwavering taste
For these dim, weathery ghosts,
And how, from the very first,
An early, innocent lust
Delighted in such wastes,
Sought with a reckless thirst
A light so pure and just.

ANTHONY HECHT

BIRTHDAY PARTY

Roomful of children,
Four-year-olds with fine bones,
Puppy-skippers,
         lithe skeletons,
Their thin domed skulls
Flying new bright hair,
Shy eyes at first,
         hanging back,
               clutching objects,
Soon all chuckle and scamper,
Five under the piano,
         one
Blindfold
     searching,
         others
Jumping because they want to pee,
Everyone wound up
With his
     or her
         intentionality
Leaping up behind curtains
Downing sausages and jelly
Stamping shreds under shrieks,
Balloon-   •
     and
         zip-
            bursting,
               silent
For a story,
         raucous at music,
Filling the room with flutes,
Guttural gnashes,
         we
            adults,

> Stunned,
> > staggering,
> > > contain the pack
> Until they are pinned,
> > > coated,
> Collected away,
> > > then in the sweet-smelling
> Debris
> > lap the calm and sigh.
>
> Still the ghosts of little girls
> Whirl and whisper with dark eyes:
> Small boy spirits
> > > punch
> > > > and
> > > > > roll
> Still under the piano,
> > > their
> Molecules of continuity in the air,
> Their thin-boned human energies
> Filling the room like flowers still,
> And us,
> > with some deep and weary
> Grateful
> > satisfaction.

DAVID HOLBROOK

PARABOLA

Year after year the princess lies asleep
Until the hundred years foretold are done,
Easily drawing her enchanted breath.
Caught on the monstrous thorns around the keep,
Bones of the youths who sought her, one by one
Rot loose and rattle to the ground beneath.

But when the Destined Lover at last shall come,
For whom alone Fortune reserves the prize,
The thorns give way; he mounts the cobwebbed stair;
Unerring he finds the tower, the door, the room,
The bed where, waking at his kiss she lies
Smiling in the loose fragrance of her hair.

That night, embracing on the bed of state,
He ravishes her century of sleep
And she repays the debt of that long dream;
Future and Past compose their vast debate;
His seed now sown, her harvest ripe to reap
Enact a variation on the theme.

For in her womb another princess waits,
A sleeping cell, a globule of bright dew.
Jostling their way up that mysterious stair,
A horde of lovers bursts between the gates,
All doomed but one, the destined suitor, who
By luck first reaches her and takes her there.

A parable of all we are or do!
The life of Nature is a formal dance
In which each step is ruled by what has been
And yet the pattern emerges always new:
The marriage of linked cause and random chance
Gives birth perpetually to the unforeseen.

One parable for the body and the mind:
With science and heredity to thank,
The heart is quite predictable as a pump,
But, let love change its beat, the choice is blind.
"Now" is a cross-roads where all maps prove blank,
And no-one knows which way the cat will jump.

So here stand I, by birth a cross between
Determined pattern and incredible chance,
Each with an equal share in what I am.
Though I should read the code stored in the gene,
Yet the blind lottery of circumstance
Mocks all solutions to its cryptogram.

As in my flesh, so in my spirit stand I
When does *this* hundred years draw to its close?
The hedge of thorns before me gives no clue.
My predecessor's carcass, shrunk and dry,
Stares at me through the spikes. O well, here goes!
I have this thing, and only this, to do.

A. D. Hope

AUTUMN'S TROUT

He must have waited years,
Staying within himself,
Earning his size under ice

In floods and summer lows.
And he must have lain there, in the dark
Of a wall, where the water cracked,

Came whipping down a chute
And turned a hundred whirling ways
At once. But his eye knew them all,

All the tricks the stream could play.
And when the light came, he sank;
When it left, he rose, a god of arcs

And muscle, a piece of darkness
Shaking free and plowing air
For bugs. Maybe ten years

Since I'd seen the place; and now,
September had climbed the year,
And old grass was in my eye.

A stream of in-between things
Was pouring through my mind,
As I cast for something like my life.

O lord, when he hit, he tore
Me loose from green, from in-between;
And for a second, the world was a line

Between us, on fire in the air.
Then he was gone, after a leap
That set me back a step.

It was enough, for the blood
Needs only a step ahead or back
To turn a certain way, to say,

Brown trout, keeper of the deepest green,
I've touched the final summer edge of you.

Harry Humes

THE MUSKELLUNGE

I'd walked past the store, stopped, then drifted back
To where the window bulged with reels,
Tapered fishing line, lures, and hooks;
And since it was November, shotgun shells,
Red hunting hats, gloves, and one stuffed owl.
So having seen that old familiar country
Rising up, I went in with some veiled hope
Of finding there some object, something
Apart from the wind and the threat of snow.

And I stood by the glassed-in shelves,
Inspecting this or that device, and once
Considered buying a knife with twenty blades
(To slash, punch, scale, or open cans of beer),
But I said no, and left it, moving on among
The fathers, sons, salesmen, feeling somehow
Out of place, as if they knew I'd come
With no good reason, making moves
I'd made too long ago, forgetting all
Except the blood-deep feel of them.
And so I came to where the muskellunge lay,
Its heart stopped by some cold play.

There I stopped, and felt its river wetness
On my face; saw its dark green back,
Deep with silence; its belly white as sleet;
And eyes unfathomable, as though a stone
Would sink in them in spirals out of time.
Even lying dead it seemed to move,
Weaving with the river, muscular and tough,
Beyond the dirty floor, the store, the stares. . . .

And I thought of that great river,
Susquehanna, like a dark vein
Flowing through this afternoon of grief:
Past the fishermen by fires huddled
On gray banks; past the faded patchwork farms;
And by the deer-and-fox-quick forest.

And for a time I saw that fish rage,
With its violent cargo of teeth,
Across the tangled waters of the world,
Prepared to rip the right whale of the flesh
To shreds, the minnow of the bone to dust.

Ah, muskellunge,
If you could tell what water weaves itself
Around you now, or what dark hunger drove
You to embed yourself on a barbed world;
Or why in death your lines precisely
Arch like sky down to the river's edge,
Then I could tell why, on a bitter day,
I felt your dead heart like the April sun
Break up the jam of sorrow's ice.

Outside, in the air, as I left the store,
Some rhythm picked up and carried
Through the flakes inexorable waves
That broke down this long afternoon,
Like heavy swirls that some great fish
Would cause in shallows, just before
It turns and glides inevitably away.

Harry Humes

THE MEXICAN PEACOCK

for Flannery O'Connor

He presses the eight-o'clock dew with sharp, short paces,
the tail, laid plume on plume, balanced over the grass
by inches, dipping not touching; the stiff, elegant
crest over the head level in motion as a queen's chin,
the ordinary toes carrying cautiously every ocellate
moon, sun, whorl, enjambment of color.

The water-lily cups have unclenched to the glitter—
white and pink still chilly, ixora and oleander
still moist—but the Mexican sun is stoked and ready.
The peacock mixes blue and greens, deepens them, pauses,
preparing to celebrate himself in an invisible glass
that kindles a blue royal enough for a *pavo real*.

You, a woman not dazzling, and cripplingly caught,
moved as swift and pitiless as light, neither more nor less,
among the pinchbeck vanities, the mingy shifts
of the heart, the small, shabby panics of the killer,
the lethal state of grace abrupt as a pitfall.
Intellect, intellect, love, and shame occupied your power.

Yet the vain, stupid, ill-tempered peacock obsessed your desire
from child to death; the unfurled arc,
the eye of glory, the tilted head of a bad bird
went straight to the center spot, the bull's-eye of mystery:
its maker's imperious pleasure in a living thing
lovely and loveless as a pausing peacock,

who pauses now, suddenly to hoist his soundless plumes
trembling and blazing in a fringy arc;
to the right he bows his crest; shudders his moons;
ignited by the sun, bows to the left.
That message of gratuitous pleasure to the beholder
in communion with our joy transfixed you.

JOSEPHINE JACOBSEN

DAUGHTERS OF MEN

How shall we face them who've so fully grown
Out of our lusts that we can not be lucid
Fronting their eyes, accusative and bold,
As words around them fall like the used leaves

Of our undercover world?
                        Who would dare warn
Or fence them in habitual wires of danger
When, our own puppets, we have danced along
The frayed nerves' tendrils pent on febrile pleasure?

Fear that in some young other they may find
How feeble was our aim, how slight our size,
Causes dismay and most dismembers. Lust
That is spent is ash: we hope for smoke

To frighten them of fire while it obscures
The very little that it's all about—
The cut and thrust, the murdered blood that's shed
To gratify an anthill vanity.

"Be frank," we say invitingly, and offer
A shadow succour to the succubus
We sense might lie in each of them, that once
Could have devoured us had it appetite.

What have we planted there but all that's mean
And witless in ourselves—like love's blind finger
Probing to penetrate the dams of passion
We half-believed, yet feared, might burst upon us

And sweep us, helpless, into utter waste?
"Beware of men," we urge, and it's ourselves
We are protective of under the covers,
Dry-thighed, sore-throated, breathing only caution.

                                 Louis Johnson

STONES

The moving of stones, that sly jockeying thrust
takes place at night underground, shoulders first.

They bud in their bunkers like hydras. They puff
up head after head and allow them to drop off

on their own making quahogs, cow flops, eggs, and knee
caps. In this way one stone can infuse a colony.

Eyeless and unsurprised they behave
in the manner of stones: swallow turnips, heave graves,

rise up openmouthed into walls, and from time
to time imitate oysters or mushrooms.

The doors of my house are held open by stones
and to see the tame herd of them hump their backbones

as cumbrous as bears across the pasture in
an allday rain is to believe for an afternoon

of objects that waver and blur
in some dark obedient order.

MAXINE KUMIN

THE BLACK SUN

And I am become death the shatterer of worlds . . .
—Bhagavad Gita

1

It was a black sun that was burning
On Wednesday
Or Thursday and it was shining
But   I was lying in a bath
I was about to drift off to sleep
The walls had just kissed me goodnight
And the water was pink as the sun set
Instead of the usual grey
But it must have been morning
I never have a bath in the afternoon
But getting back to what you said
I can't really remember who
It was that put that black sun there

2

When the time came
It was as if we had been waiting
Sitting here all the time
There was little sound
Hardly as much as the ship when you sailed
You said it would be for a little time
And not to worry
So you left us all waving
And the sound rolled in about six that morning
A soft rolling thunder that lulled us from our sleep
And then we saw the fishes
Opening their stomachs to the air
And we saw the green sea eat them
And the sea grew red as the light grew red
And we saw the sun

WHEN THE SUN HAS DIED

Life and dreams are leaves of one and the same book.
—Schopenhauer

As the earth cooled the sound of margays came
Over the wind slit by omens and your dress
Twisted around your ankles on the hilltop,
An old-time Liberty/Angel half-turned;
Weathervanes looking frantically for the cause
Squealed on their rods, in Kansas possibly
Sensing a twister, till your crutches came
Carrying you back to the porch and the wind died.

"No one wants to be told it; if you must,
Get to the county seat and wait in the square,
Stand and pretend to grudge a glance at the dusk
As if it came upon you and touched you
Like petals that jostle your manhood in the spring.
To sit, lame, and look through a yellow album
And wonder could there be a home if it
Were otherwise, to wake without sleeping...."

So many times I imagined leaving you
That once I pictured a black road going north
So vividly I have not returned from it.
Creak of a rocker following, flumes, gorges
Passing like torn scrap paper and your iron heart
Beating behind me like a war party,
At last I reached a place with a heated spring
Coming directly out of the earth's core.

There the alfalfa was a little green
As warmer land melted the thick frost.
From granite hills we watched the sun and moon
Equal in light and heat rising and setting.
The last birds circled across us—was it still
Hotter in Kansas? A lapidary worked
His hours nine to five in the grim cold
And cut his semiprecious into cubes

In which so very much was locked away
That hallucinations rose in them like clouds.
I saw an American farmhouse weathered well
And lived in through maternity and death
Till the white wood took on a cast like stone,
A place we have been away from too long
To know the names and recognize the stones
Till all the fire left us at half-noon.

He kept the hours and the small shop-bell
Was silent—only in sonic booms
As war-planes vaguely hunted for a war
It tinkled slowly, or when I came in
And we looked each other in our frozen eyes,
I saw these memories and prophecies
Like a manuscript somehow gotten out of order
Or margays calling in a Kansas night.

David R. Lenson

Our daughter liked the place. The blackboard in her room,
she wrote and talked upon it by the hour,
playing school, I thought, and then I found
she talked to you, the chalk dry on her tongue,
a duster ready in her hand to rub you off.

I broke a tarata leaf between my fingers;
the clear scent reminded her of you.
She grows tall and straight, is liked by people,
as far as I can judge. Most of all
she lacks confidence. She always did.
I'll get in touch with you again.

JACK LASENBY

REPORT TO YOU

Are you there still, in that house of dark and light?
I went back once and looked, but strangers ate
fruit from our trees, they didn't know your name,
hadn't seen you. But where else could you be
where else could you dance except between
the lemon and the fig tree—wine on the table—
where else could you go, where could you dance?

Falling in love with witches was too easy.
New leaves on the fig, big as my palm,
green as puriri moths, light from the house,
and a witch dancing on the damp spring lawn.

Your hawk still ticks in my brain. If I take off
his hood, he'll hook out both my eyes,
but he must be wound or my heart will stop and stop
remembering you, and where else could you dance?

When you come in, nails clicking across
the hard floor, breathing clay, tugging
the edge of night, I shall warm a little milk,
pour it in a saucer by the door.

The tree we planted between us grew to the sky;
our fingers lost touch round its trunk.

Our third Christmas without you. Our daughter grows.
She's much taller, got most of her second teeth.
Last year's school report's the best she's had.
She still wakes at night and stands by my bed.
What else would you like to know, that most of all
she needs you, has too much of me?

Last year we lived in a house with a ngaio tree
at the top of some steps, a flax bush out the back,
and on a lawn behind, a lemonwood—tarata.

LOSING YOU

Another summer gone,
the hills burned to burdock
and thistle, I hold you
a moment in the cup
of my voice,
you flutter
in the frail cave of the finch,
you lean to speak
in my ear
and the first rains blow
you away.

Dusk is a burning
of the sun.
West of Chowchilla
The Lost Continent of Butterflies
streams across the freeway.
Radiators crusted,
windshields smeared with gold
and you come on
rising into the moons
of headlights.

My brother is always a small bear,
cleaning his paws,
I am a leopard
running through snow,
you are the face of an egg
collapsing sideways.
Now the last olive falls
gripping its seed
a black stone among stones
and you are lost.

In a white dress
my little girl goes to the window.
She is unborn,
she is the thin flame
of a candle,
she is her mother
singing a song.
Her words frost
the mirror of the night,
a huge wind waits
at the back of her breath.

     Philip Levine

SURVIVAL STORY

    Tonight I sleep
with no stiletto knife under my pillow
for from hot guns which spill blood I am safe.
I walk the world armed with intelligences
that others do not possess
and have been educated towards success.
I travel and am widely respected.
My friends are similarly marked
and together we eat and drink
while others claw for bread and water.
My children are bright as tristars
and read literature late into the night.
This house is mine,
it came with smiles and handshakes
which is the civilized way.
On this earth I am assured of long life
and am welcomed in banks and insurance palaces.

    Three thousand years ago
I would have been expert with flint
and an organizer of wood collections
for the big fire at the cave's mouth.
Wild beasts would have run
from the glare of my defences.
I would have taken three, four wives
and my sons grown rosy on pig-fat.
We would have hunted snake where the swamps start.
By my summer sea-cave I would have
speared the stupid fish,
and slept each night where the earth
was moulded to the shape of my body.
There would have been no bone knife
under my pillow of lamb's skin.
I would have lived long in a wild land
and been mentioned in epic poems.

Now,
    as then,
reports reach me of plans to review my status.
Also there are rumours of death.
But still I am secure.

    Nothing has changed.

WES MAGEE

LIGHTNING BUGS

We used to take an old lamp with the bulb out
And a steel wire from a milk bottle top
Twisted and stuck in the lamp to make contact
And run it out to the hogwire fence
When they were rising like static around us
And electrocute the lightning bugs in a shower of sparks.
Great power flowed in the current of our hands
As we probed with the electric tip of our minds
For whatever it was in the core of light
That burned all day in the heart of things
And rose in the night, in the dazzling darkness,
And swarmed from the shadowy forms of the earth
Like pulses of thought—the white, elliptical ghosts
Of trees, the fiery tip in each blade
Of grass, and the pastures rising above themselves,
All in their own true forms at last,
Like the souls of the just. And we were plugged into
It all we believed and flowed with a power that leaped
In invisible arcs from the static swirling of stars
In space and the flames of unknown galaxies, down
To our illumined heads and out the sockets
Of our eyes along the wire to the fiery fence,
Where the bugs we impaled turned crisp and died,
Oozing their liquid jelly of light
While we turned green as fox fire, our hands
And mysterious fingers, even the hair and grain of our skin
Streaked and smeared with gleams of solid light.
And then, then we stalked through the dark of our childhood
Like *ignes fatui* following the luminous forms
Of ourselves, grim as ghosts haunting our bodies
Back to the blinding effulgence of home.

FRANK MANLEY

POEM

1

For months I've walked this rocky coast,
building my fires in windless cracks,
snaring my birds from the air, fish
from the gray sea. One net for all,
flashing into the element.

I carry my wife inside me.
I bear my children in the wave's hiss.
I swim with the porpoises, naked
and shining, my hair close to me.
The whale sings me his long song.

On land I am flaky. Bits of me
break against stone. The wind looks after
my loosening hair. This falling
apart is my daily miracle.
Night is alive in another place.

2

I am never far from edges.
Here, the land pushes into the sea
and up, as always, into the air.
The white eyes of the sea open
and close like stars everywhere.

I sleep on my arm, rise with it
bloodless, dragging against me, hold
it under the fire to bring it back.

I am not alone. Everything
speaks. Each wave is a tongue. Each stone
is a language rolled into one.
The weeds are dialects of wind
and water.

I will go back some day. Winter
is hard in these caves. The sand stings.
Summer is better, though barely.
I lie on the low rocks where land
and sea come close to each other.

3

This is the time before time.
The waves are one continuous
roar, the wind a single breath, birds
the feathers of the one body.
Light is a version of sight, the heart stone.

This is the sea without stop,
the rolling thorn that grows to itself.
This is the sky holding itself
in its cloudless arms.
This is.

4

I lie on the hot sand for hours,
watching, my head in the dune grass.
Down on the beach they are dancing,
shadows staggering among flames.

The sea makes silence like a noise.
It never stops. The dancers fall,
exhausted, laughing. They think they are drunk.

They smell of meat, salty and burnt.
Even now, they know what they want.
It lies on them sleeping like dew.

The fire falls, at last, like shadow.
Into itself.
The hiss whose silence is its voice
licks us into darkness.

5
The whales have drifted away,
having seen. The wind sucks at my ears.
The sea, too, looks at me sideways,
wrinkling away, through its single squint.
It is time to go back.

The sky's eye rolls in its juices,
milky, looking for its own pupil,
looking for the other eye, lost,
on the far side of its head,
the eye that can see for itself.

ROGER MITCHELL

THE SKIN

Under the hot sun today
I saw the shed skin
caught among dead grass-stalks
sun-blonded by springtime,
stubbled by drooling mouths
of passing beasts.

Without looking to see who was about
I carefully lifted the colourless skin,
fearful that its faintly marked
diaphanous brittleness
might crumble in my hand
or break of its own weight.
Then I laid it out beside me
on the fallen tree-trunk.

Here were the eye-markings,
high up on the blunt diamond of the head
in which the shape of the mouth opened
as if in a snarl of defiance, and there
was the slim tapering towards the tail,
the tip moving, as if in life,
with the touch of the breeze.

For a time I sat looking at it,
the shed skin with the faint markings—
the head, with shape of eyes and outline of mouth,
the straight body,
the quivering tail.

Then I took it up
(with no wish to flinch from its touch)
and rolled it into a ball,
tenderly feeling its brittleness
break into pieces in my hand
and collapse of its own weight.

Next I hid it under a bush
lest someone passing see it there
and despite the heat of the sun
should shout "A snake! A snake!
A snake has shed its skin here.
It can't be far away;
come quick, bring sticks and stones;
find it and break its evil back;
hang it over the wires of the fence
so the kids can throw stones at it
until it dies at sundown."

Then, having hidden it,
the slim tapering skin with its faint markings,
now crushed into an ugly lump
the colour of dirty milk,
I tossed a small twig
down into the gully.

"Hey, you there," I shouted,
"you in the fine new shining summer skin,
it's good to think there's something
left alive on earth
since before the time of man."

But not until I first
had looked all around,
up the road and down,
and across at the distant houses,
to make sure
no one would hear me.

Ian Mudie

A SMALL WAR

Climbing from Merthyr through the dew of August mornings
When I was a centaur-cyclist, on the skills of wheels
I'd loop past the Storey Arms, past streaming lorries
Stopped for flasks of early tea, and fall into Breconshire.
A thin road under black Fan Frynych—which keeps its winter
Shillings long through Spring—took me to the Senni valley.

That was my plenty, to rest on the narrow saddle
Looking down on the farms, letting the simple noises
Come singly up. It was there I saw a ring-ousel
Wearing the white gash of his mountains; but every
Sparrow's feather in that valley was rare, golden,
Perfect. It was an Eden fourteen miles from home.

Evan Drew, my second cousin, lived there, a long, slow man
With a brown gaze I remember him. From a hill farm
Somewhere on the slopes above Heol Senni he sent his sons,
Boys a little older than I, to the second World War.
They rode their ponies to the station, they waved
Goodbye, they circled the spitting sky above Europe.

I would not fight for Wales, the great battle-cries
Do not arouse me. I keep short boundaries holy,
Those my eyes have recognised and my heart has known
As welcome. Nor would I fight for her language. I spend
My few pence of Welsh to amuse my friends, to comment
On the weather. They carry no thought that could be mine.

It's the small wars I understand. So now that forty
People lock their gates in Senni, keeping the water out
With frailest barriers of love and anger, I'd fight for them.
Five miles of land, enough small farms to make a heaven,
Are easily trapped on the drawing-board, a decision
Of the pen drowns all. Yes, the great towns need

The humming water, yes, I have taken my rods to other
Swimming valleys and happily fished above the vanished
Fields. I know the arguments. It is a handful of earth
I will not argue with, and the slow cattle swinging weightily
Home. When I open the taps in my English bathroom
I am surprised they do not run with Breconshire blood.

LESLIE NORRIS

BEACHMASTER

His mother from the loving sea
Lurching, found him by smell,
Although the nursery beach
Was thick with milk, and other
Blubber. Her comfort was all
Tacky liquid and the touch

Of nuzzle and rubbery flipper.
Weak and thin at first, he was
Afraid of water. But grew
Lusty, casting in plump sleep
His long, white, birthday fur.
In a ring it lay. He was

Left miniature sleek seal.
After three weeks she abandoned
Him, the call of heavy bull
In the sexual tide and swell
Being too much, though he moaned
With his pup's silk mouth the whole

Of a day. That night he snarled
At the spray and set off.
In ten weeks such a pup, in
Its first green diving of
The seaways, untaught, alone
In bottle-coloured water,

Swam six hundred miles, to Spain.
That was not my pup, though he
Savaged fast shoals in places
Far away, and dragged his growing
Awkwardly over other beaches.
This is his country, where young

Cows come out to call him home
And meadows of the sea swing
Miles deep under him. Here
He first fought, nostrils popping
In muscled water, in fury
Of instinct, for a territory.

He keeps ward offshore, armour
Of scar thickening shoulder
And neck; hulk bull, upright
In lull. Nobody sees him eat.
On the loud beach his sons, small,
Weak, wait for white fur to fall.

LESLIE NORRIS

BRIDGES

Imagine the bridge launched, its one foot
Clamped hard on bedrock, and such grace
In its growth it resembles flying, is flight
Almost. It is not chance when they speak
Of throwing a bridge; it leaves behind a track
Of its parallel rise and fall, solid
In quarried stone, in timber, in milled
Alloy under stress. A bridge is

The path of flight. A friend, a soldier,
Built a laughable wartime bridge over
Some unknown river. In featureless night
He threw from each sliding bank the images
Of his crossing, working in whispers, under
Failing lamps. As they built, braced spars,
Bolted taut the great steel plugs, he hoped
His bridge would stand in brawny daylight, complete,

The two halves miraculously knit. But
It didn't. Airily they floated above
Midstream, going nowhere, separate
Beginnings of different bridges, offering
The policies of inaction, neither coming
Nor going. His rough men cursed, sloped off,
Forded quite easily a mile lower.
It was shallow enough for his Land Rover.

I have a bridge over a stream. Four
Wooden sleepers, simple, direct. After rain,
Very slippery. I rarely cross right over,
Preferring to stand, watching the grain
Of running water. I like such bridges best,
River bridges on which men always stand,
In quiet places. Unless I could have that other,
A bridge launched, hovering, wondering where to land.

LESLIE NORRIS

OLD VOICES

First the one bell, heavy, behind it
Centuries of controlled certainty, swung
With an enormous sound past
The kneeling city; it is the first
Heard stone in an architecture of ringing.
And sung in at built intervals, at
The joint of locked structure, the voice
Of the second bell. The foundation is

Set on unimpeded air. An age
Of cut stone and iron—those old
Technologies—has its immense medieval
Tongues bellowing again. Now all
The small bells filigree and stretch
A long nave in the ear and a pulled
Spire of sailing clamor. Resonant
Cathedrals of listening are launched

On the open day. But bells are not
Peaceful; are arrogant with the complete
World of their origin. Think, imagine,
In the clack of swords they began,
Short on their own shields the flat beat
Struck, so that erratic courage set
Hard in the metal; then the high edge,
Turning in the urgency of the charge,

Rang through the skulls of wives
At their keen mourning. Hacking the bent
Angles of helmets, rough blades cracked again
The wombs that bore these splintered heads
In their early down. From such sounds,
From the held quiet after, the brazen
Complexities of the loud tower grew.
There was time for the patterns of victory.

And space on the fat plains of grain
For building of flawless bells. The lost
In their slate hills had tongues only,
Grew old in the slow labor
Of changing myths. Through the mist
Of altering voices their stories spun,
Through generations of telling. Spiral
Images from the belfries, the metal

Confection of chiming, are not
For the mountains. Old men tell
Of an impermanent peace, a fragile
Faith is passed through the narrative
Villages in syllables of live
Whispers. Foolish now to regret
Centuries of locked exile. It happened.
We have heads full of easy legend

And elegies like the cold sun
Of treeless autumn. I carry
Such tunes in my head like the thin
Silence the bells hang in. But from
These reaching fields my surnamed
Fathers came, the great cathedrals
Counted them. I walk their lanes,
My shoes cover the concave stones

Worn by their slow tolling.
If I speak with the quick brooks,
Of the permanent hills, in my saying
See hordes of the dark tribes stand,
Their faces hidden, my hand
In its perfect glove of skin holds
Other ghosts. We step the streets
Uneasily, disturbed by bells.

Leslie Norris

A VALUE OF THE ABSOLUTE

Q: *Did you know it was the Devil's book when you signed?*
A: *No. But I thought it was no good book.*
   —Mary Warren's Examination in Salem Prison

Evil, too, has its good old days:
Like when you rode a broomstick to the place
And signed the Black Book in your blood
And then danced around the altar fires
And maybe drank of something hot as Satan's hoof.
And everything you touched just shrivelled up
And blew away like you held a fist of winter-kill.
And you felt yourself so lost and lonely and damned
You could turn yourself into an everlasting scream
With no sound and no echo.

Today you ride a 707 to San Juan or somewhere postcard blue
And sign the register—pastel, privileged, under smiles.
Then go dancing until the sun rolls off
And have a Rum and Coke, maybe four or five;
Then satin sex, guaranteed by this morning's pill.
Maybe get up, shower, gamble till dawn
While everything you touch turns to gold,
Including the lady you came with.
And you feel yourself so lost and lonely and damned
You could turn yourself into an everlasting scream
With no sound and no echo.

The point is simply this: in the good old days you knew someone *cared!*
Enough to pull the wishbone of your soul.
And you could always shed one last molten tear
Walking through the fine, volcanic ash
Toward your burning.

HARRY W. PAIGE

SØREN

The lion was his father,
  Apostate in the cage—
    A matted tail that swung
The mangy genitals
  Like severed fists; from these
    He saw that he was born
A moral hunchback. Fear
  Was everywhere, for fear
    Was thinking anyone
Might care for him, might love,
  Making him estimate
    His worth over again,
Even from the beginning—
  He who had no beginning—
    Force him to leave that room
Whose windows he had carved
  With his own hands, the door
    That only he could pass through,
The corner cot of straw,
  The lighthouse lens erected
    Gleaming in midfloor, naked,
The crate of notebooks scratched
  With clawmarks of Jerome's
    Blond beast, and marked *pariah*.
How leave those windows, marvels
  Of flawed glass, wart and wave,
    Each figure in sea change,
Tiding to petals through
  Disease, so that his eyes
    Wanted none, needed all,
Clawing gold from the canker—
  Hath nature fashioned well shafts
    Around roses, or planted

Roses in well shafts? And
   Who can uproot her dream
      Save he who dangles head-
Down in the cool dark column
   Of dead air, even where
      Narcissus died, and feels
The arrow from the god
   Sweet in his own flesh as
      He gazes at the buds
Sprouting in wall chinks—he,
   Who knew the god would shoot
      Sure as he bended down?

                    JOHN PECK

THE BEAUTIFUL ACCEPTANCE

Glory to those who are not afraid of disaster,
Who at the uncertain moment will place all they have won
In hazard, aware that the odds are only human
Despite successes

And that, as Mallarmé said, one throw of the dice
Will not abolish chance. Pyrrhus, when he saw
The street grow narrow behind him, the gateway blocked,
Fresh reinforcements

Struggling in to help him when he wanted
To retreat, the alien city alarmed,
Attacking from every direction, his own men
Wounding each other—

A nightmare worse than his worst dreams—
Did not look around for a bargaining position,
For the necessary betrayal, for a quick abdication.
Knowing nothing

Of the enormous veneration of life and property,
Considering the fall of cities and kings
Glorious, he took off his crown and rode out
Into the enemy.

The beautiful acceptance of the unavoidable,
When history takes on flesh and becomes an ambush:
To give off life as fire gives off light,
Consumed at the limits.

Asking for nothing but by a bitter insistence
To overcome shame with straightness of heart, refusing
All consolations. The world at any moment
May become translucent.

RICHARD PEVEAR

FOR J., ARDEA OCCIDENTALIS

1

You still sometimes sleep
inside that great bird,
flopped out,
one wing tucked,
the other slightly broken over my back.
You still fall asleep before I do.
You still wake up
in tears.

You have what is called *thin skin*:
if I put my ear to it
I can hear the wingbeat in your heart.
I can only imagine
how far down those long flights go.

2

Last night in my dream
about the heron
I stood at the edge
of water with a handful
of stones.
I was twelve, I think.
The heron perfect, still, kneedeep,
looking at himself.

Once he lifted his wings
in a mockery of flight.
For a moment I was inside you;
I could hear the heart.
I had stones in my hands.

STANLEY PLUMLY

"OLD MAN MAD ABOUT PAINTING"

From impulse challenge or defiance
Hokusai raised a great fifty-foot
framework of bamboo and red tissuepaper
higher than medium-sized pagodas
and painted his thoughts on the thing
along with mountain landscapes
releasing the slow drip-drip of water
and shrieked Eureka at the stars
                    in Japanese of course
                           the wind
came by to wreck his paper canvas
during the Hour of the Rat
Everyone thought he was a damn fool
the ricksha boys made wisecracks
and the charcoal burners razzed him
the beggars made faces behind his back
the saki drinkers kept right on drinking
the money lenders said he was a bad risk
and small boys continued the count-down
                one-two-three-four before
the monster painting slowly toppled
into the dust
It kind of cheers me
during my own Hour of Despond
when I've failed at everything
scribbling poems on the reverse side
of cost schedules scrounged from wastebaskets
to think of Hokusai in bleak poverty
before he painted a still-life of all Nippon
in the encyclopaedic Mangwa Sketches
and Thirty-Six Views of Mount Fujiyama
to think of that earlier idiotic painting
reared on momentary impulse
nobody understood but Hokusai himself

And sometimes I can actually see
the monster fifty-foot tick-tock
of paper visibly falling into the dust
without money value or the least permanence
but the fractional god of now defeated
and perceptibly merges with forever
I am beginning to understand a little
about the reverse side of mountains

                                          AL PURDY

LOVE IN AN EARTHQUAKE

When the big Seattle earthquake spoke
to our hill in a voice so deep our houses
bowed and scraped, you ran for the out-of-doors
but I caught you and held you bravely, me, the laird
of a home that quakes, and therefore stays, together.

Oh we had a cozy year I guess in the doorframe
where the building inspectors say always to go
and I thought I had finally saved a life
after a lifetime of trying
and perhaps if you'd been a stranger-girl
you'd have kissed me, and I'd have taken you in.

But my dear such flat heroics!
If I'd known then as I know now
your plumb heart my world turns on,
your graces that simply make it go—
I'd have let you dance right out on the rollicking
street in your dangerous joy, and skip
barefooted the flipping electrical wires
and sway with our neighbors' undulant chimneys—
I'd have seen you once at least in your earthquake freedom
with the sun jumping all over heaven for you
and the hill rolled back at your feet.

JAROLD RAMSEY

THE GOOSE-GIRL

Goose-girl
I must know
I need to tie it together
tight as a noose not
let it run out behind me any more

need to know
where the string ends
the ball in the palm of your hand
that was yellow
and red and blue
as you strolled on the opposite
page from Snow White

—There were windmills inside
the ball—she said
all running backwards
the yarn had spent itself
by the third turn of the river
by the gingerbread house

still I needed more
I used up my sandal straps
my belt
the ribbon that held my braid

and my hair all of it

finally my veins
weaving them together temporarily
with willow wands and moss

they unravelled too the thread
was all gone
expended extraneous irrelevant
the reel finished
like an aria snipped in two—

Goose-girl
now I remember
you came at last to the end
the secret crease
in the palm of your hand
that led to your heart it ended there

Everyone heard it break
and was sorry

and followed you crying aloud for magic

        CAMPBELL REEVES

VOICES AT THE EDGE OF THE MIRROR

    The surprise a son makes in the arms—
like hummingbird wings in the spine.
    Back home alone in the house I peel
the stale clothes, bone-tired, ready to flop.
A hard first birth for Anne, eighteen hours
of labor, but finally done.
    Deep above our roof, clouds of stars
comment the night. Mysterious clarities
of seed-fine script, puzzling the eye.
    The blue metal hands of a clock
tick thin as razors. The refrigerator motor
pulses our empty rooms till they hum the ear—
as of a plane seeping away: high, distant.
I stare into a wall that reflects me
strange with fatigue, and think of my father
crashed in New Guinea jungle
                            before I was born.
    His green mold bones sloshed down long ago.
Or still fuselaged perhaps in the crumpled Grumman.
An aluminum wad, a thickening clutch of vine.
    The bedroom's thin, still whir. Family voices
pool at the edge of the mirror, a family face
in my own sperm looks out from the glass.
                      Generations
coming down through the darkness; their stir
of hummingbird wings in the blood.

                                        Reg Saner

A SUICIDE PACT

The rope is asking *Why?* from its mild white room.
Swinging aimlessly, it drifts in arcs which narrow
To circumscribe a head, yellow, white, grey, with red
Bruises, before it passes on to another livelihood.
The rope smelled stale in its coils in the closet;
It was taken from a shelf of dishes and slipped
Over the hands it holds by a nail to the ceiling,
Sliding upon the floor, making musty conclusions
Of a man's face ajar, its remembrance of motives
Opening outward like the eyes of the condemned.

Is this knowledge: that he too once walked naked,
The sphere his own haven, dangling from a rope?
He climbed it, hand after hand, emerging into a pure
Historical era—and time grew fast around him like
The premeditated goal of two people coming together
To create an abundance of willing flesh. Only
The change is not so miraculous: it is deadening
Enough to prevent the reaching out for unseen gifts,
The dependence at last on charity, the emergence of
Torturing instruments indulged until they too die.

Heaven help him, but he does fragrant penance,
Of nothing less than the trespass into the territory
Of the glad gods: a man is made beast—as if
To love between those two kinds were impossible.
And his attendance danced upon the loftier aspects
Of a life lived well before such divorce: he worried
About debt in an emergency, though he need not have
Been exposed to such indignity. Apparently stable,
A credit to his house, he lost her—driving through
Relentless traffic on the way to the hospital.

Against property, the accumulations of a life,
And the woman whose body he found split asunder,
He collected himself into a quiet room, bulbs hanging
Above, in deep space, the surface of a dying dust.
And the glistening body of love breaks, spilling
Over, passing along the margin of conscience intact,
Like an uncertain umbrella over an unwarranted lie.
And her body's debris, floating pale in the light,
Drifts down to complacent explanations of the day—
As if the act of death alone were an abasement.

And how the thick rope over his future plans soared:
For then, missing her, secured from himself behind
His locked door, regretting nothing at all of the past,
Everything he owned, he thought of it hidden below
On the shelf, as in a deep sleep. And, ascending it
Knuckle by knuckle, his thoughts entered an aura
Of listening: he beheld, like a flag woven of pain,
The woman's face then—he pressed it in his arms.
His hands, the hands of years ago, clutched at the air:
How could he pass the barrier of their separate desires?

And all those forgotten staircase landings left
So suddenly incomplete—see how wretched they are:
A hole in the face of a solitary house—it leaks
As a window slides open, filling with water. But then,
As his simple voice once simulated gentleness,
Would he have been better off left alive alone? . . .
Once upon a time a little boy listened at the casement
For a story, then crawled out into the starry night.
He never heard another sound. He climbed close to her
As he himself was hanged, become a better man.

DAVID SCHLOSS

SCORPION

Under its stone, it pleats
and unpleats ebony, it digs
a bed which is a body-print
exactly, room for pincer, tail
and sting. If it elbows out, it leaves
cold accurate evidence of its tenancy.

Bedded with it, less precise,
the ambling grubs and slow-worms
eat and burrow deep sometimes
as earthworms, not disturbing that
fast eel of their element—for it
has eyes or nerves that flinch

malignantly at a grain's shift.
I follow you hunting with jar and trowel,
with gloves, this poison tail.
Each time you turn the right stone up—
warm flat stones which roof
an airless square of dark

and hold all night the sun's warmth
for the black king-pin of the poor soil.
The stone raised, the creature poises
tense and cocked. Tail curled, it edges
forward, edges backward—its enemy
so big he is invisible (though a child)

hunched over it, who trembles too
at such a minute potency.
And you flick it with the trowel
into the jar, where it jerks and flings
its fire in all directions at hard
transparency. It asks no mercy.

You bear it to an anthill,
tip it on the dust. Like a cat
it drops right side up, into a tide
of sharp red pincers. It twitches
its tail to a nicety and twice
stings itself—to death. Piece by piece

it is removed underground by the ants—
a sort of burial—perhaps to be
reassembled as a kingly effigy
somewhere deeper than we care to think,
bound homeward with our empty jar:
and the field, full of upturned stones.

MICHAEL SCHMIDT

LESSON IN SURVIVAL

To stay good currency with your heart solvent,
Be a pink bus-ticket used as a bookmark,
A maidenhair fern, pressed but eloquent.

Look for a hidey-hole, cosy or dark,
Where no peekaboo finger or eye can excite
A meddlesome bigwig to poke and remark.

Survival is mostly a matter of oversight;
Be an old pencil stub, a brass curtain ring.
Don't keep your lid screwed on too tight.

With luck, your neighborhood fairy will string
You along as a glass bead, a silver key,
A saved blue feather from a jay's wing.

A person like you, a person like me,
Must contrive to find butter, but not too much jam;
Live happy and warm as a pick-a-back flea.

Don't be a new airport, the flag of Siam,
A battleship decked with bunting and trouble,
A three-volume novel, the Aswan High Dam,

To founder in foundries of smoke and pink rubble,
To swell and topple, absurd, indecent,
To puff and froth like an overblown bubble.

Be a bit too precious to throw away, spent;
Be good for others, or perhaps a lark.
Be a whispered name, not a granite monument.

PETER SCUPHAM

NATIVITIES

A breed nagged by the urge
to look in on its own beginnings
could settle for worse than this:
the garden, the three
creatures hatching the batch of woe
that fell on us all.
It has the merit of somebody
to blame the evil on;
it has the kind of cast we understand —
hero, girl, rapscallion.

As if nature still tried for titans
we get every so often the news
of a remarkable infant.
The clod centuries keep flowering
into these super babes,
which means not only that eternity
with its tail in its mouth won't do,
but that when it comes to the first
thing that occurred,
we'll put carts before horses
to make it a birth.

Pick among magicians, dismembered
Brahma, Plato's dividing eight-limbed beast,
the rib or the ash tree. We'll accept these.
But tidal ooze and stellar explosions
leave us cold. They're too impersonal.
The event begs for characters
only the miracle can furnish.

Though it's not enough that a wand was waved
and something popped or clicked.
There remains the yen
for the irrational *mise en scene:*
the impossible two leaning over
the nest with the first egg in it.

R. E. SEBENTHALL

FLYING FROM DUBLIN

The white beam from the tower sweeps round and round
And each plane spins a red beam on its top
As one might swing a berry on a thread;
But far from being little silver trout
The monsters in this dim aquatic landscape
Seem sharks waiting to glide off after prey.
But how link flight with fishes? Flying fish
Skim on the surface like spun discs of silver
Then dive into their liquid element;
But these pale fish with stiff unmoving wings
Will climb the air, eager for space and height.
They turn the world to maps, the sea to leather,
The land at night to clusters of bright beads.
These strings and trails and curves of coloured stars
Outline whole cities with their myriad lives,
Each life a dot, yet each a complex network
Of loves and links and cares that give dimension.

Seasoned highflyers stroked with stock politeness,
We are not fooled about the truth of danger.
But birth itself is danger: paper walls
Are all that keep us, all our lives, from death.
Wingless or winged, we can but launch ourselves
On life as on the buffetings of air.
Booked on unscheduled flights with unknown destinations,
How trustingly we travel to our end!
Well, we have company and more than musak
And plastic food to nourish and divert us.
As travellers we need the bird's eye view
Without forgetting sharks that lurk below.
Arrivals and departures are unending:
The painful, joyful journey is all we know.

JOAN MURRAY SIMPSON

DOWN, DOWN

I am says the bulldozer
Singing brighter than the birds
A thousand birds on a thousand branches
Sing no merrier than I

And the crickets' *alas*
The brittle scraping
Of a million legs together
Or the bellowing of frogs.

I am and send my weighty message
Over the hills at daybreak
Breaking hills
I am stronger than the mountain.

I push up the knotted roots of sycamores
A hundred summers gathering
I shake the sunflowers
Where the spotted eggs are hiding.

I stamp down this terrace. I descend
To the Pleistocene. This was a lake
Then rock. I make it a meadow.
No ages for me. An afternoon is enough.

I am says the bulldozer
And compassed round with music.

ANN STANFORD

CHILDREN'S GAMES

for Evan and Margot Jones

Except for the way they've made the town their own,
   you might suppose them truly the last
and the best of savage tribes. Their burgher fathers
   have vanished before their time, the mothers
may still be home but are neither seen nor heard,
   yet the place drums with life. The world
is given into unpractised hands; the exercise
   of these and mine and now has fallen
to the beings for whom a broken lath is tragic,
   the notion of death comic. Their seeming
is almost what they are, as they bump and haul
   and bundle one another through
a space naive and public, and a time
   told purely on the pulses. Round
and round they process and swing, as round
   and round go hoop and keg. The few
who recede up stream or street do not succumb
   to the long, proportioning view; and the boy
who clambers up a tree as if away,
      climbs, he knows, a mast, a spire,
         the one tree in the world.

"Women make us poets, children make us
   philosophers": but who made these
the sovereign players they turn out to be?
   No lank barbarian, no beast,
languid and charging by turns, is any emblem
   for these in their civility.
You see it in their poise, in the spinning tops,
   the broom balanced by hand, the stilted
stride, the two ferrying a third,
   and in the dissembling: a child in a mask
gazes down at the scene, another goads
   a fractious hobby-horse across
the square to Heaven or Haarlem, the gamblers shuffle,
   a stormed hillock becomes a fortress.

And most of all, amidst a kind of humorous
   vehemence, they intertwine
in a great sociable game. The genial tumult
   averts the chaos we affect and fear,
the bleak autistic dream where each one mimes
   a shade's memories of a shade's dreams,
   and charms us back to sunlight.

The night will come, in Flanders and the rest,
   the toys be left or lost. Gravely,
these children will manoeuvre and assuage,
   will give up hoodman-blind and hunt
for loves, acheivements, candles. The girl who can't
   dance will say the band can't play,
the boy find shafts are heavier on a cart,
   music will tremble in their parching throats,
and not descend from the spheres. But still
   a memory will lodge in their bones.
the sway of corn danced upward from the ground,
   of wild prey summoned to range,
of rain invoked from the clouds. They will be clad
   in mud-caked jerkins, weighing serge,
and yet be haunted by the gusty flare
   of gold autumnal vestments, still
be decked with ancient hopes. The man who hefts
   sod for a polder, the woman pale
in childbirth or in charges, will remember
   sweetness in movement, light in season,
   a dear human stand.

PETER STEELE

THE DEAD AND THE LIVING

At Crowland it is easy to remember the dead.
Low sunlight lifts a stone-cross to your face.
Snow falls expectedly through the abbey's roof.

At this far end of day it is common to feel
sly shadows of long-boats darkening the Fens.
In low-lit seasons such hauntings are usual.

Stones here are cenotaphs—smashed columns that frame
a monotonous landscape. What they say
make you think of the dead living under the dead.

I think today of those unknown living who died.
Armies that went down into a foreign desert.
Bones that rest now under chaotic airports.

I think of the dead where only the trees grow.
Where snow falls on long dismissed footprints.
Where no stones remember their ruined seasons.

I think of the unknown dead under today's living,
under new office blocks and expensive hotels,
under the roadways and new city pavements.

I think of those unliving faces of women
searching for looks in a junk-shop of mirrors,
hiding their fears in a graveyard of wishes.

At Crowland it is easy to remember the living.
Snowlight brings your eyes down to a stone.
Under death's open roof we share the same epitaph.

Edward Storey

CELLAR

That time I tumbled into the dark—
  tilt, plunge, and cry
  through a trap door left open
  in a trusted pantry floor—

     that descent, child hair streaming,
     into a kingdom of potatoes
     (their tall eyes sprouting upward
     like pale green rockets),
     dried onions, squash, a squeak of cabbages,
     carrots hanging like withered darts,
     preserves and relish winking
     from provident shelves,
  but the dust alive, and daintily clawed;

     that moment of plunging through linoleum
     embossed with faded birds
     (the bitter smell of wind
     or coal or something darker
     hunched inside a box),
     the gasp of arrival on hardened earth,
     then the quick leap up
     the black wood stairs
     toward a living room with lights still on—
        being saved from rot
        and breathing mice
        and the crimson stars of tomatoes sliced
        and staring out of glass—
     resurrected, full of heart . . .

but now on deeper nights
a different void
below the edge of things—
the humpbacked dreams, the whirring sweat,
and no light left
except a bedroom clock's dim hands
that pace my foolish,
                climbing breath.

                ADRIEN STOUTENBURG

From
ELEGY FOR MY FATHER

Robert Strand 1908-68

1. THE EMPTY BODY

The hands were yours, the arms were yours,
But you were not there.
The eyes were yours, but they were closed and would not open.
The distant sun was there.
The moon poised on the hill's white shoulder was there.
The wind on Bedford Basin was there.
The pale green light of winter was there.
Your mouth was there,
But you were not there.
When somebody spoke, there was no answer.
Clouds in the blind air came down
And buried the buildings along the water,
And the water was silent.
The gulls stared.
The years, the hours, that would not find you
Turned in the wrists of others.
There was no pain. It had gone.
There were no secrets. There was nothing to say.
The shade scattered its ashes.
The body was yours, but you were not there.
The air shivered against its skin.
The dark leaned into its eyes.
But you were not there.

2. ANSWERS

Why did you travel?
Because the house was cold.
Why did you travel?
Because it is what I have always done between sunset and sunrise.
What did you wear?
I wore a blue suit, a white shirt, yellow tie, and yellow socks.
What did you wear?

I wore nothing. A scarf of pain kept me warm.
Who did you sleep with?
I slept with a different woman each night.
Who did you sleep with?
I slept alone. I have always slept alone.
Why did you lie to me?
I always thought I told the truth.
Why did you lie to me?
Because the truth lies like nothing else and I love the truth.
Why are you going?
I don't know. I have never known.
How long shall I wait for you?
Do not wait for me. I am tired and I want to lie down.
Are you tired and do you want to lie down?
Yes, I am tired and I want to lie down.

5. MOURNING

They mourn for you.
When you rise at midnight,
When you rise and the dew glitters on the stone of your cheeks,
They mourn for you.
They lead you back into the empty house.
They carry the chairs and tables inside.
They sit you down and teach you to breathe.
And your breath burns, it burns the pine box
And the ashes fall like sunlight.
They give you a book and tell you to read.
They listen and their eyes fill with tears.
The women stroke your fingers.
They comb the yellow back into your hair.
They shave the frost from your beard.
They knead your thighs.
They dress you in fine clothes.
They rub your hands to keep them warm.
They feed you. They offer you money.
They get on their knees and beg you not to die.
When you rise at midnight they mourn for you.
They close their eyes and whisper your name over and over.

But they cannot drag the buried light from your veins.
They cannot reach your dreams.
Old man, there is no way.
Rise and keep rising, it does no good.
They mourn for you the way they can.

6. THE NEW YEAR

It is winter and the new year.
Nobody knows you.
Away from the stars, from the rain of light,
You lie under the weather of stones.
There is no thread to lead you back.
Your friends doze in the dark
Of pleasure and cannot remember.
Nobody knows you. You are the neighbor of nothing.
You do not see the rain falling and the man walking away,
The soiled wind blowing its ashes across the city.
You do not see the sun dragging the moon like an echo.
You do not see the bruised heart go up in flames,
The skulls of the innocent turn into smoke.
You do not see the scars of plenty, the eyes without light.
It is over. It is winter and the new year.
The meek are hauling their skins into heaven.
The hopeless are suffering the cold with those who have nothing to hide.
It is over and nobody knows you.
There is starlight drifting on the black water.
There are stones in the sea no one has seen.
There is a shore and people are waiting.
And nothing comes back.
Because it is over.
Because there is silence instead of a name.
Because it is winter and the new year.

MARK STRAND

OMEN

You will not even notice our departure.
The small, falling like plump leaves
among the fallen leaves,
will lie indistinguishable, each with his song
locked in his throat.
The large, unable to climb, to soar,
will invisibly die in their high places,
which only the few sure-footed among you could scale.
Only the tame, safe in your cages, will, for a time, survive.

We have, it would seem, outlived our purpose,
whose strokes in the sky taught you symbols
to preserve what you thought.
In those days, we seemed lines drawn by a wise god
as we flew, flocked,
presaging more than a change in season.
Each savior in turn had his holy bird,
his practical, heavenly messenger descending
to peck a seed from the ear or to seal some voice as divine.

We, who announced the birth of each sun,
who once were, to the discoverer,
true sign of the unseen,
longed-for land ahead, now may announce no new thing
save this darkness
which we, at your bidding, must enter.
We fall, as pit-birds fell, silent.
Their silence was always clear warning to you to turn back.
But you, hacking at shadows, still fail to hear us though we cease to sing.

Jon Swan

THE HAND

It was a hand. God looked at it
And looked away. There was a coldness
About his heart as though the hand
Clasped it. As at the end
Of a dark tunnel he saw cities
The hand would build, engines
That it would raze them with. His sight
Dimmed. Tempted to undo the joints
Of the finger, he picked it up.
But the hand wrestled with him. "Tell
Me your name," it cried, "and I will write it
In bright gold. Are there not deeds
To be done, children to make, poems
To be written? The world
Is without meaning, awaiting
My coming." But God, feeling the nails
In his flesh, the unnerving warmth
Of the contact, fought on in
Silence. This was the long war with himself
Always foreseen, the question
Not to be answered. What is the hand
For? The immaculate conception
Preceding the delivery
Of the first tool? "I let you go"
He said, "but without blessing.
Messenger to the mixed things
Of your making, tell them I am."

R. S. Thomas

OVER ELIZABETH BRIDGE:
A CIRCUMVENTION TO A FRIEND IN BUDAPEST

> . . . *my heart which owes this past a calm future.*
> Attila József, *By the Danube*

Three years, now, the curve of Elizabeth Bridge
Has caught at some half-answering turn of mind—
Not recollection, but uncertainty
Why memory should need so long to find
A place and peace for it: that uncertainty
And restless counterpointing of a verse
"So wary of its I," Iván, is me:

Why should I hesitate to fix a meaning?
The facts were plain. A church, a riverside
And, launched at the further bank, a parapet
That, at its setting-out, must swerve or ride
Sheer down the bulk of the defenceless nave,
But with a curious sort of courteousness,
Bends by and on again. That movement gave

A pause to thoughts, which overeagerly
Had fed on fresh experience and the sense
That too much happened in too short a time
In this one city: self-enravelled, dense
With its own past, even its silence was
Rife with explanations, drummed insistent
As traffic at this church's window-glass.

How does the volley sound in that man's ears
Whom history did not swerve from, but elected
To face the squad? Was it indifference,
Fear or sudden, helpless peace reflected
In the flash, for Imre Nagy?—another kind
Of silence, merely, that let in the dark
Which closed on Rajk's already silenced mind?

Here, past is half a ruin, half a dream—
Islanded patience, work of quiet hands,
Repainting spandrels that outarched the Turk
In this interior. These are the lands
Europe and Asia, challenging to yield
A crop, or having raised one, harvest it,
Used for a highroad and a battlefield.

The bridge has paid the past its compliment:
The far bank's statuary stand beckoning
Where it flows, in one undeviating span,
Across the frozen river. That reckoning
Which József owed was cancelled in his blood,
And yet his promise veered beyond the act,
His verse grown calm with all it had withstood.

CHARLES TOMLINSON

László Rajk, Hungarian Foreign Minister, executed during the Stalinist period; Imre Nagy, Prime Minister and leader of the 1956 revolution, also executed. The poet, Attila József, killed himself in the thirties.

THE POSSESSED

The strength in me is not mine.
Not anybody's. It is too much
For one heart to hold, for one
Mind to make welcome here
In the world where strength is a strange thing—
Listen. This is not me talking,
Not even the wind, not even waves
Breaking. What you hear and see
Is the truth coming through, the iron
Entering, then lingering, then
Leaving on its terrible errand
To others, who will know it is not
Their own, it is so strong, so strange,
So cruel; and beautiful past bearing.

Mark Van Doren

AFTERWARDS

Afterward, we quarrel from love
And once again we are back
In our disparate bodies.
The room cools, almost darkness,

My fingers gripping the fallen quilt.
You lie as if at the edge of the sea,
The sun gone off the water.
Hair has the slipperiness of eelgrass.

Oh, the words you flung, I hear them,
Pebbles tumbling, smoothened with use;
But hurting; but individual; belonging
To us—worth keeping for themselves.

While you sleep, I gather them.
You shift. I listen for the city.
Tire-hiss, a draining breakwater;
I remember finding a kittiwake, dead.

You are so cold. I should cover
This illicit skin awash in the moon.
I lift you as though you were mine
To keep. Let me see your eyes.

TED WALKER

CHILDERMAS HYMN: DECEMBER 28, 1970

while we were waiting for Andrew Michael Robert Riter

1

Out of egg grease, burned at the bottom of the pan
Out of the calendar, newspapers, coffee stain
The child is born
At the death of the year, a child is born

That is why we bring a tree into the house:
Because there were two in Eden
Now we hang silver spheres from the branches
And lights, to show this is the Tree of Life
We know that if we could only hold the fir up against the sun
A child on fire would break out between its gleaming needles

In the darkest season. From stomach cramps
From black rage, meanness, pettiness
Out of cracked cups, and milk powder
The child is born

That is why we choose holly, that blooms at midwinter
Sharp-leaved, for the pain
The child comes out of pain, comes covered in blood
Red as the holly-berry, with a dizzy sickness

At the coldest time. In the wet snow
Out of fighting the traffic, hating your work
Out of nothing to live for
A child is born
At the death of the year, a child is born

2
This is why we sing, this is the miracle
Why we ask shepherds dead two thousand years
Why they are suddenly happy
Why we gather together and fill our mouths
With joy like new cake, like candles
There is roast turkey and drink
We relax around the amazing sight:
A tree brought into the house and decorated
Under the tree we put gifts for each other
Bright with red and gold paper
Tinselled, shining, ribbons of white and green
Crinkly blunt packages, neat boxes

Because of the child
Because of the child, kings appear out of the East
Because of the child we become kings

3
Though we will not win
Though the mother separate from the father
One daughter dislike the other
Though we are on welfare, without money, nothing to give
Though the future is laundry and babyshit
Though children are born at the edge of the field, between
    the work of the rows
Though there is a fire made to adhere especially to the flesh
    of the newborn
Though flesh be born cooked and bones drool

Still we celebrate
For this we forgive sins, for the year child
This is how we leap through, clean
To the new world, the child, the following year

Though there is new brocade in the house
Though we are rich with laughter, nuts and oranges are in
    bowls
And everyone is full

4
Praise, then
Praise for the mother, for this mother
She is not lazy, here is her house
Out of a darkness, love has grown
Until her face is the sky every day
Praise to her. Let music surround her
She is the Queen of Heaven, in her sweat and glory

Praise to the child: the Sabbath queen, the king of the Jews
Praise to the child, princess of mercy, prince of peace
Praise to the child who comes, he is the family

A child is born
At the death of the year, a child is born
Light the tree

Tom Wayman

BEFORE THE NIGHT

One poet tells us
of blinded children beating
at their eyes, perhaps to strike
the sparks from them of light
burnt out.
        And another
is much moved to make a poem
out of a report that H. D.,
having a stroke, fiercely desires
to communicate
                and "strikes her
breast in passionate frustration
when there is no word at her
tongue's tip."
        No word,
no word wherein before one's
heart was satisfied, a jetting
out as of a fountain, fire,
lute.
        No word, no sight;
one beats against the wall,
be it blindness, be it flesh,
the body
             turned to stone
against the wish that Lazarus-
like would rise.
              As she, a lovely
poet once, now, at the end
of sight, those children
at the start, haunted by all
the light
           that they were cheated

of, beating, beating, trapped
birds, prisoners in their
own bones, the midmost of the
night.
   An awing light in this
for us who still can see and see
the blinded priestess, writhing,
racked, on her enormous sight.

THEODORE WEISS

READING THE RITES

Not for the lately dead, but for these
In the pit-site of a desert excavation,
Newly turned to light at pick's point,
Fish-hooked in the empty eye
And brought up for the reading of bones:
So many with yaws, so many cases
Of caries, rickets, so many arthritic hands,
Joints, spines, so many osteosarcomas
Told by the bones; so much accumulation of pain
In a midden, passed out of being
With the contents of skulls, past feeling
Except to these hands that turn the ancient sand,
Carefully turning the last rigidities
Of knotted bone, counting their ills.
What their own priests once said for them lost,
Lost in the tongue they said, yet
Not to be turned under again before some rite spoken,
Some pit-side prayer for their broken rest made
To the bone-reader's God, who walked with men
In the day of these bones, in another desert,
Counting the stricken, and promised an end
To ills, a place of wholeness, his heal to pain shared
By these bones now reading and the bones lately read.

Nancy G. Westerfield

BEGINNINGS

for my mother

1

In my grandmother's house
A chaleh baking,
A tiger cat rubbing against the cellar door,
The stove in the middle of the room,
The fish smells boiling . . .

My mother's face as a girl, sweet, compelling,
Large black eyes, plump freckled cheeks,
Pimples she thinks are boils.
Her small breasts dent the pocket of her cotton blouse;
She breaks stringbeans in a pot
And dreams . . .

My grandmother stands at the oven baking,
She tends the plants in the garden,
She feeds fine leftovers to her fifteen cats
And week-old bread to the sparrows and jays;
But she forgets
The quiet girl musing in the corner
Wishing a man's strong hands
Would open her blouse
And press her thighs
So tight her heart screamed.

At the table's head sits my silent grandfather, tense, forbidding—
Among the large-bearded uncles, the busy men,
He eats his meat without sound.
      Nothing rustles but the wind under the tablecloth,
         Nothing sighs.
My grandmother's hands knead dough,
My uncles talk of politics and school,
(Will the White Guards win? Will Trotsky lose?)
And my grandfather, worn with work,
Looks like the prophet Isaiah
Under his peaked workman's cap.

2

Outside a man is waiting.
He is tall and large and dark;
His thick hands clasp and reclasp,
His face is filled with the restless ardor
Of the ignorant, passionate poor.
He talks of carving fortunes
From the sombre rocks of Manhattan,
Of wresting gold from granite so hard
The mica won't flake out.

My grandmother mutters. My uncles gibe and taunt.
But the dark man lingers—
At night in the sunroom
He fumbles tender words.
In the hallway his eyes gaze
At the girl's soft breasts, at the woolen skirt
That sticks to her legs—
He opens her checkered blouse
And breasts flow out like pigeons
Cupped in his calloused palms.

3

And now my birth is told
In halls beyond the skyscrapers' peaks
(Sorrow comes slowly, like dawn
Through dark green shades);
I remember the arguments,
The words, the words,
The newspapers ripped and thrown to the floor
(We are bitter in our poverty
Perched high on the cliffs of hard Manhattan
Far beyond Central Park)
    Is Trotsky bleeding? Is
    Beria dying?

DATE DUE			
RETURNED 1974			
DEC 0 5 1983			

DEMCO 38-297